T0028540

 ESSENTIAL HISTORIES

The Hundred Years War
1337–1453

Anne Curry

OSPREY PUBLISHING
Bloomsbury Publishing Plc
Kemp House, Chawley Park, Cumnor Hill, Oxford OX2 9PH, UK
29 Earlsfort Terrace, Dublin 2, Ireland
1385 Broadway, 5th Floor, New York, NY 10018, USA
E-mail: info@ospreypublishing.com
www.ospreypublishing.com

OSPREY is a trademark of Osprey Publishing Ltd

First published in Great Britain in 2023

© Osprey Publishing Ltd, 2023

The text in this edition is revised and updated from: ESS 19: *The Hundred Years'
War: 1337–1453* (Osprey Publishing, 2002).

Essential Histories Series Editor: Professor Robert O'Neill

All rights reserved. No part of this publication may be reproduced or transmitted
in any form or by any means, electronic or mechanical, including photocopying,
recording, or any information storage or retrieval system, without prior
permission in writing from the publishers.

A catalogue record for this book is available from the British Library.

ISBN: PB 9781472857064;
eBook 9781472857095;
ePDF 9781472857088;
XML 9781472857057

23 24 25 26 27   10 9 8 7 6 5 4 3 2 1

Cover design by Stewart Larking
Maps by The Map Studio, revised by J B Illustrations
The images on pages 55, 97, 99 and 128–129 are available under CC BY-SA 2.0:
https://creativecommons.org/licenses/by-sa/2.0/
The image on page 77 is available under CC BY-SA 3.0: https://
creativecommons.org/licenses/by-sa/3.0/
Index by Zoe Ross
Typeset by PDQ Digital Media Solutions, Bungay, UK
Printed and bound in India by Replika Press Private Ltd.

Osprey Publishing supports the Woodland Trust, the UK's leading woodland
conservation charity.

To find out more about our authors and books visit www.ospreypublishing.com.
Here you will find extracts, author interviews, details of forthcoming events and
the option to sign up for our newsletter.

CONTENTS

vo raulme de france fut depuis monlt
affoibli someu de puissance et de
conseil / Et sachiez que se les anglois
eussent chacie ainsi quilz firent a
poitiers encores en feust trop plus de
mours et le roy de france meismes
mais nennil Car le samedi onques
ne se partirent de leur convoy ne
chacier apres homme / Et se tenoyent
sur leur pas gardant leur place
et se deffendoient a ceulx qui les as
sailloyent / et toit se sauua le roy de
france a destre / Car le dit roy demou
ra tant sur la place asserprees de se
ammemrs sicomme cy desfus est dit
quil fut monlt tret / et quil nauoit
apres departement quisplus de se bo
mes que buns que autres. Et adonc
le prist messire Jehan de haynaulx par
le frain qui lauoit en garde et acon
seilles et qui la lauoit remonte une
foiz / Car On trait on auoit occis le co
sier du roy et lui dist sire tenez bous
en si se est tempo ne bous perdez mye
Cy simplement Se bous auez perdu
ceste foiz bous recouueres une autre et
lesmmena le dit messire Jehan de har
nault comme par force  Si bous
ay que ce iour les archiers Danglere
porterent tyant confort a leur partie
Car pru leur trait les cusreurs dict
que la besongne separfist combien quil
y out bien aucuns bailloos cher de
leur couste qui baillanment se com
batuent de lamain et qui monlt y fist
belles appertises darmes et de tyant
recouuance mais on doit bien sen
tir et congnoisstre que les archiers yst
vent tyant fait / Car pru leur trait
de commencement fuirent les tyeue
noys desconsis qui estoyent bu obyg
qui leur fut bu tyant auantaige Car

troy tyant foyson de tyene darmes sicie
ment armez et praez et bien montez / Ainsi
que on se montoit adonc fiuent desconfis
et perdiz par les tyeneuors qui trebuschoxt
parmy eulx et sen coulloyent tellement
quilz ne se pouoyent leuer ne mouion Et
la entre ces anglois auoit pillaux et chr
baulx gaillois et cornillois qui pour su
uoyent les tyene darmes et auchiers qui
portoyent tyans coutilles / Et senoyent
entre les tyens darmes et leurs archiers
qui leur suruoyent boye / Et troinoyent
ces tyens darmes en ce doncher contes
baruns chlds et escuiers si les occioyent
sans mercy com tyant fire quil feust par
cest estat on y out ce soir plusieurs perdiz
et murdriz Dont ce fut pitie et donma
ge / Et dont le roy danrletevrre fut de
puis courronucie que on ne les auoit pa
a rancon Comment le roy danrletevrre fist
nombree les mors et puis sen parti de creq
et bint iusques deuant calaix et comment
le roy de france setourna a paris

INTRODUCTION

The Hundred Years War is a term invented in the 19th century for the late medieval conflict between England and France, although the actual war lasted for 116 years, from 1337 to 1453. England and France had been at war on several occasions before 1337 because of the tenurial relationship of their rulers. The kings of England were dukes of Aquitaine, an important area of south-west France from which most of England's wine supplies were drawn, but they were not sovereign there, as they held the duchy as a vassal of the king of France. What seems to mark out the war that started in 1337 as different is that it involved a claim by English kings for the crown of France. Edward III had started putting forward his claim after the death of Charles IV of France in 1328, on the grounds that he was the nearest male relative of the late king. Edward's mother, Isabella, was Charles's sister.

Historians have long debated the seriousness of Edward III's intentions when he formally declared himself King of France at Ghent in 1340. Did he really intend to make himself king? Or was he merely trying to use his hereditary rights as a *potential* claimant to the French throne as a bargaining counter, to win a breakthrough in the disputes that had plagued him and his predecessors over their French lands? This possibility seems to gain validity by the fact that Edward did give up his title 'King of France' in the Treaty of Brétigny/Calais of 1360 in return for a generous territorial settlement in his favour. Given Edward's apparent willingness to abandon the title, can we take seriously his resumption of it in 1369 when Charles V of France reopened the war by exploiting loopholes in the treaty of 1360? The English did so badly over the next 30 years that it is hard to see the claim as anything more than an empty insult to the French.

OPPOSITE

Edward III viewing the French dead after the battle of Crécy, from a copy of Jean Froissart's *Chroniques*, made in Paris c. 1410. (Den Haag, Koninklijke Bibliotheek)

King Henry VI of England was crowned King of France in Notre-Dame de Paris on 16 December 1431, shortly after his tenth birthday. (Niday Picture Library / Alamy Stock Photo)

Yet Edward III's successors, Richard II, Henry IV and Henry V, did all call themselves King of France and were all involved in conflict with France. Did they have as their principal war aim the crown of France? Was this what prompted Henry V's celebrated invasion of 1415? If so, why was he prepared to give up the title at the Treaty of Troyes in May 1420? But why, too, were the French prepared to accept him at that moment as heir and regent of their ruler, Charles VI, thereby disinheriting Charles's own son (later Charles VII) and paving the way for a double monarchy of England and France – a prospect as remarkable at the time as it might seem to us now?

As it happened, Henry V died a few weeks before Charles VI in 1422. Thus it was his nine-month-old son, Henry VI, who became king of both kingdoms. He was crowned as king of England at Westminster Abbey in November 1429, and as king of France at Notre Dame in Paris in December 1431. His crowning might suggest that the English had won the Hundred Years War. But the victory was short-lived. Neither a treaty nor a coronation could make the French accept a ruler who was king of their bitterest enemies.

In 1429 the tide began to turn, partly as a result of the triumphs of Joan of Arc, which add a remarkable and still not wholly explained dimension to this stage of the Hundred Years War. By 1450 the English had been expelled from their last remaining strongholds in Normandy, and in 1453 Gascony also fell. Only Calais, taken by Edward III in 1347 in the wake of his victory at the battle of Crécy in 1346, remained in English hands, hardly enough to justify the retention of the title 'King of France'. Yet English kings did retain this title down to 1801, two and a half centuries after they lost their last toehold in France – Calais – in 1558.

The Hundred Years War raises many problems over the war aims of the English kings and of French responses to them. It is also an intriguing war in military terms, not least because of what it suggests about the development of infantry and artillery, which some historians have deemed to constitute a veritable 'military revolution'. The Hundred Years War contains many different styles of warfare: naval and terrestrial; sweeping, long-distance *chevauchées* (mounted raids); systematic conquest and occupation; 'set-piece' sieges and battles, as well as short, sharp periods of *blitzkrieg*; small-scale skirmishes and 'unofficial' raiding and piracy. Although it was fought predominantly in France, England was itself a theatre because of raids on the south coast by the French and on northern England by their allies, the Scots.

LE TRESVETORIEVX ROY TE FRANCE

CHARLES SEPTIESME TE TE NOM

Portrait of King Charles VII of France by Jean Fouquet, 1445, now in the Louvre, Paris. (Photo by Fine Art Images/Heritage Images/Getty Images)

There can be no doubt, too, that the Hundred Years War plays a fundamental part in the formation of both England and France as nation states. Taxation developed in order to finance the war. The demand for an effective military machine helped to create complex administrative structures and moves towards standing armies. There is nothing like a war, especially a long-drawn-out one, to promote a sense of awareness of national identity and unity. With English governments frequently reminding their subjects that the enemy French were intent upon invading and destroying the English tongue, it is not surprising that this tongue should be extolled, and the sense of Englishness thereby enhanced. Although wars in this period were still basically caused by, and fought over, the rights of *kings*, there can be no doubt that the Hundred Years War was waged between the peoples of both kingdoms, not least because the rulers made it so.

A hundred years is a long time, even in the medieval period where, without the benefits of modern communication methods, events took longer to be known outside the area in which they had occurred. Whilst we can identify broad themes and long-term consequences, it is also essential to emphasize the various phases of the war. But even this disguises the momentous changes in the fate of whole nations which might occur as the result of one event – not least, for instance, the few hours on 19 September 1356 which saw the capture of John II at Poitiers, and led to the English triumph in the Treaty of Brétigny/Calais of 1360, or the murder of John the Fearless, Duke of Burgundy, on 10 September 1419 by the Dauphin Charles's supporters, which led to Henry V's acceptance by Charles VI as heir and regent of France in the Treaty of Troyes of 1420.

At a more local, small-scale level, individual French villages might well regard the brief but often cataclysmic passage of English troops or of the free-booting *routiers* as their defining moment of the Hundred Years War, the kind of microcosmic detail that is necessarily lost in a book of this length. The aim here is to provide an overview of the war as a whole.

BACKGROUND TO WAR
England and France at peace and war: 1259–1328

Enmity between the kings of France and England arose because of the landholdings of the latter in France. These were at their greatest extent between 1154 and 1204 when the Angevin kings of England (Henry II, Richard I and John) ruled Normandy, Maine, Anjou, Touraine, Poitou and Aquitaine. By 1224, during the reign of Henry III, all these areas save Aquitaine had been lost to the French. The Capetians had conquered the lands by exploiting their feudal overlordship.

The Angevin kings of England were not sovereign in their French lands but held them as vassals of the French king. This situation was reinforced by the Treaty of Paris, which Henry III made with Louis IX in October 1259. Henry surrendered his claims to all the lost lands in return for confirmation of his tenure of Bordeaux, Bayonne and their hinterland known as Gascony, and the promised reversion of other areas of the old duchy of Aquitaine, most notably Saintonge to the north of the Gironde, and Agenais and Quercy on the eastern frontier, as well as rights in the three dioceses of Périgueux, Cahors and Limoges. As some of these areas had been in French hands for over 50 years, boundaries were disputed and allegiances were doubtful. A further complication was introduced when the county of Ponthieu, the territory around the

mouth of the Somme, came to the English king in 1279 through Edward I's wife, Eleanor of Castile.

The most important aspect of the Treaty of Paris of 1259 was that it confirmed the vassal status of the English kings, obliging them to pay homage to the French king for their continental lands. Henry III set the precedent, kneeling before Louis IX in the garden of the palace on the Ile de la Cité, close to the newly constructed Sainte-Chapelle.

The gilt-bronze tomb effigy of Eleanor of Castile, Queen of England (d. 1290), on her tomb in Westminster Abbey. (Photo by Angelo Hornak/Corbis via Getty Images)

THE LANDS OF THE ENGLISH KING AS CONFIRMED BY THE TREATY OF PARIS, 1259

Ile d'Oléron

POITOU

Saintes

LIMOUSIN

Vienne   Limoges

— · — · Approximate boundary of the Duchy of Aquitaine in 1307 according to the evidence of the Gascon rolls

SAINTONGE

Medoc

Blaye

Bourg

Périgueux

PERIGORD

Isle

Fronsac

Libourne   Castillon (1453)

Bergerac   Sarlat

Bordeaux

Dordogne

GASCONY (GUYENNE)

La Rèole

St-Macaire   Marmande   AGENAIS

Bazas

Lot   Cahors

St Sardos
Aiguillon (1346)

QUERCY

Garonne   Agen

ARMAGNAC

Baïse

Gers

Tartas

Dax

Aire

Bayonne   Auch

BEARN   BIGORRE

N

0   25 miles

0   50 km

And for what he shall give us and our heirs, we and our heirs will do him and his heirs, kings of France, liege homage, for Bordeaux, Bayonne and for Gascony and for all the lands that we hold beyond the English Channel ... and we will hold of him as a peer of France and as Duke of Aquitaine. *(Treaty of Paris, 1259)*

Homage was due at every change of monarch on either side of the Channel, and was renewed in 1273, 1285, 1303, 1308, 1320 and 1325, albeit often reluctantly on the part of the English king. The latter – sovereign in his own kingdom, yet a vassal in his continental dominions – was at a disadvantage. His French overlord could hear appeals by his own vassals against his rule and could summon him to his court in Paris.

The last quarter of the 13th century saw the theory and practice of kingship develop by leaps and bounds on both sides of the Channel. Edward I of England (1272–1307) sought to assert his sovereignty over vassal rulers of Wales and Scotland. Philip IV (1285–1314, also known as Philip the Fair) attempted to extend his royal authority over his subjects as a whole and over his major vassals, in particular the king of England and the Count of Flanders, ruler of a rich and highly urbanized area in northern France with important trading links with England. Thus, just as war had broken out in 1202 when Philip II (1180–1223, also called Philip Augustus) declared John's lands confiscate, so wars arose between Philip IV and Edward I in 1294, and between Charles IV (1322–28) and Edward II (1307–27) in 1324 in the same way.

The war of 1294–98

Both these wars arose out of charges trumped up by the French. Philip encouraged appeals from Edward's vassals in Aquitaine. The actual *casus belli* arose from disputes between sailors of Normandy and Gascony, culminating in an attack on La Rochelle by sailors from

Bayonne in May 1293. In October, Philip summoned Edward to answer complaints against his Gascon subjects and officials. His non-appearance and the failure of negotiations led to the confiscation of the duchy in May 1294.

The French were already well prepared for invasion. After a series of successful sieges, Bordeaux itself fell, although Bourg and Blaye held out, being assisted by an armed fleet from England. Bayonne also fell briefly but was also recovered, thenceforward becoming a base for raids into the Languedoc towards Toulouse which have similarities with the *chevauchée*-style activities of the Hundred Years War. Toulouse was one of several bases where armaments were being gathered. In 1295, Philip even planned an invasion of England.

These are not the only ways in which the war of 1294–98 presages the Hundred Years War. In both, the defence of Gascony relied on the inhabitants of the area, and relatively few English troops were sent. Edward I did not fight in Gascony in person, choosing instead to campaign in Flanders, much as Edward III was to do later. Indeed, no king of England went to Gascony throughout the whole of the Hundred Years War.

Secondly, although the war of 1294–98 was not dynastic, it showed that Anglo-French war had to be waged on a grand scale, as a conflict between monarchs with much pride at stake. Thus costs were immense even though the actual war was short. Philip spent at least 432,000 *livres tournois*, perhaps 61.5 per cent of his income for 1294–98. He tied up large sums in sieges and occupation of castles, many of which changed hands with alarming frequency, much as they were to do after 1337. Edward spent around £400,000 – all of his regular and taxation income. He had to have recourse to a very heavy customs duty, the *maltolte* (evil tax), facing much criticism. He desperately needed funds to repay loans – as with his successors, there was never enough ready cash. The nobility opposed his demands for military service when he was not campaigning in Gascony in person. Thus at Ghent on 5 November

OPPOSITE
The Tour du Grand Port in Libourne, a fortified town in Gascony named after Roger de Leybourne, lieutenant of Aquitaine 1269–1272. (Photononstop / Alamy Stock Photo)

Philip IV was followed on the throne of France by three of his sons, Louis X, Philip V and Charles IV. His daughter Isabella married Edward II of England. (Album / Alamy Stock Photo)

1297 he was forced to reissue Magna Carta and to abandon the *maltolte*, confirming the need to have parliamentary approval for the levy of taxation, a major turning point in English history.

> Henceforward no aids, mises or prises will be taken from the kingdom except by the common consent of the whole kingdom and for the common benefit of the kingdom.
> *(Edward I's agreement of 5 November 1297)*

Thirdly, Edward I sought to divert Philip by campaigning in northern France with the aid of alliances of Low Country and German princes eager to be paid for their military services, and often with their own axes to grind against the French. Flanders was particularly ripe ground for this strategy in the late summer of 1297. A similar policy was adopted by Edward III in the early stages of the Hundred Years War, and the negotiation of alliances remained a major feature throughout the conflict.

There is a further 'international' area where the war of 1294–98 set the scene: the development of the Franco-Scottish link, the 'auld alliance'. Indeed, it was because Edward I tried to impose his lordship over Scotland by summoning John Balliol, whom he had chosen as king in 1291, to provide military service, that Anglo-Scottish relations broke down and that a Franco-Scottish treaty arose in October 1295. From this point Edward was also at war with Scotland, a war that dragged on inconclusively into the next century. Whilst some advances were made, these were lost under Edward II when the Scots, now under the rule of Robert I (Bruce), defeated the English at Bannockburn (1314), an important victory for infantry over cavalry, and began to launch raids into England. It was already clear that Anglo-French wars would not simply be a straight fight between these kingdoms.

The sting was taken out of the payment of homage to the French king by Edward I bestowing the duchy on his son, Edward, Prince of Wales (later Edward II). It was the latter who paid homage in 1308, and whose marriage to Philip IV's daughter Isabella was intended to cement peace between the two sides. At this stage, no one could have envisaged that this marriage was to lead to its offspring, Edward III, being in a position to claim the crown of France. Philip IV had three sons – Louis, Philip and Charles – thus the French succession seemed unproblematic.

The war of 1324–27

The war of 1294–98 exacerbated the problems of sovereignty and territory. There were also new disputes, not least over the restitution of lands that had fallen into French hands between 1294 and 1303. A conference was held at Périgueux in 1311 but to little avail. Pressure on the frontiers of the English lands continued. These factors contributed to the outbreak of another war in 1324.

Again, the war was provoked by the French. Charles IV's officials encouraged the abbot of Sarlat to build and fly the French flag at the *bastide* of Saint-Sardos in the

The English Royal Family

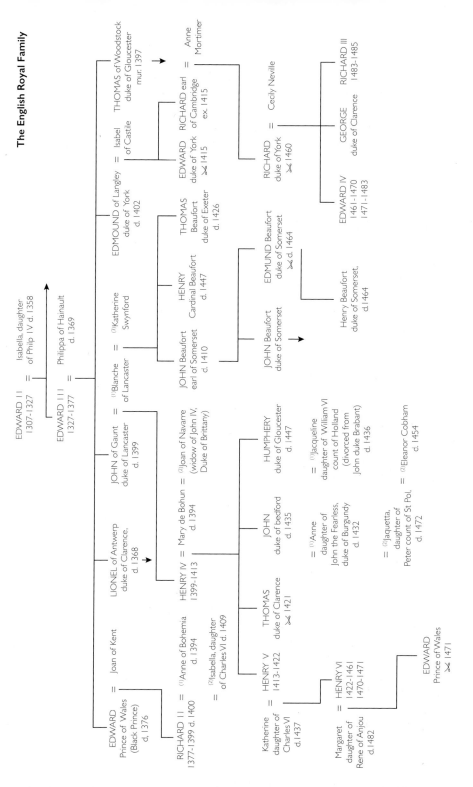

Agenais, an area technically under English rule, but which had been disputed since the war of 1294. Charles was perhaps anticipating that the English military response would be constrained by commitments in Scotland. The English seneschal of Gascony, Sir Oliver Ingham, took the bait. He attacked the *bastide*, allowing Charles to summon Edward to his court, and subsequently confiscate his lands.

Charles IV himself journeyed down to Toulouse – a rare visit of a French king to the south – where the nobility of the Languedoc gathered in arms in his support. Ponthieu fell without resistance. The French took the Agenais and laid siege to La Réole. The war cost the English much less than that of 1294, but there was marked expenditure on defensive engines at Bordeaux aimed at keeping enemy shipping at bay. The French took few places in Gascony thanks to local forces aided by English and Aragonese troops.

Actual war was conducted for only 15 months. In October 1325 Edward, Prince of Wales (the future Edward III), accompanied by his mother, paid homage to Charles at Paris. Whilst negotiations continued, Queen Isabella returned to England with her son and engineered the deposition of her husband in January 1327. This was facilitated by the armed support of John of Hainault, acquired through the marriage of his brother the count's daughter, Philippa, to Prince Edward. This link was to be important in Edward III's search for allies at the outset of the Hundred Years War.

In February 1327 the English were still urging the seneschal of Aquitaine to recruit Aragonese troops, whilst the French were considering plans for a full-scale invasion of the duchy. An interesting document survives in the papers of one of Charles IV's councilors estimating that a 14-month campaign would be required, and that the cost could be over three times the annual average income of the French crown. It would be impossible, therefore, without exceptionally heavy taxation, a problem that beset both sides throughout the Hundred Years War. But what is significant is that

the French were contemplating the complete removal of the English only a decade before the Hundred Years War began.

The deposition of Edward II in June 1327 and the accession of his son at the age of 14 made it difficult for the English to avoid agreeing to peace terms not in their favour. The French were in no real position to conquer Gascony, but they still had the military upper hand: even as negotiations went on, sieges were being conducted along the Dordogne. The peace of Paris agreed in March 1327 and proclaimed in September forced the English to pay a war indemnity of 50,000 marks as well as a relief of 60,000 *livres tournois* for the duchy, for which the future Edward III had already paid homage in 1325. Worse still, the Agenais remained in French hands, as did the area around Bazas. Disputes over the lands of dispossessed Gascons dragged on inconclusively.

OPPOSITE
At Ghent on 26 January 1340 Edward III formally announced his claim to the throne of France, assuming the quartered arms of France and England which were borne by his successors down to 1801. (Bibliothèque Nationale de France)

England, Scotland and the French crown

In the meantime, the English attempted to renew their war against the Scots who had invaded northern England, but they failed to defeat them in Weardale in July 1327: the English campaign was marred by a violent dispute between John of Hainault's company and English archers. Under such circumstances, Edward III and his advisers had little choice but to agree to another humiliating settlement, this time with the Scots. On 17 March 1328 at the Treaty of Edinburgh (confirmed at Northampton in May) Edward surrendered 'any right in Scotland which we and our ancestors have sought in past times in any manner', thereby recognising Robert I as King of Scotland without requiring any homage.

Into this scenario came a new issue, the succession to the crown of France. Charles IV died on 31 January 1328. All had to await the birth of Charles's posthumous child (1 April 1328). This turned out to be a girl. An assembly had already decided in February 1317 that women could not succeed to the kingdom of France. (This decision had been occasioned by the potential inheritance of the daughter of Louis X, who was passed over in favour of her uncle, Philip V.) Thus there was little debate in 1328. Women could not inherit the French throne,

PHILIP III 1270–1285 = Isabel of Aragon

PHILIP IV 1285–1314 = Jeanne of Navarre

CHARLES count of Valois and Anjou d. 1325 = Margaret of Anjou

PHILIP VI 1328–1350 = Joan of Burgundy

JOHN II The Good 1350–1364 = BONNE of Luxembourg

LOUIS X 1314–1316 = (1) Margaret of Burgundy
= (2) Clementia of Hungary

PHILIP V 1316–1322 → (2 daughters)

CHARLES IV 1322–1328

ISABELLA 1292–1358 = EDWARD II King of England 1307–1327

EDWARD III 1327–1377

JEANNE Queen of Navarre d. 1349 = PHILIP count of Eveux

JOHN 1316

PHILIP count of Longueville d. 1363

CHARLES I King of Navarre d. 1387

CHARLES II of Navarre

BLANCHE d. 1392 = PHILIP duke of Orleans d. 1375

CHARLES V The Wise 1364–1380 = Jeanne de Bourbon

LOUIS duke of Anjou d. 1384 →

JOHN duke of Berry mur. 1416 →

PHILIP The Bold duke of Burgundy d. 1404 = Margaret daughter of Louis de Mâle. Count of Flanders

JOHN The Fearless duke of Burgundy mur. 1419 →

ANTHONY duke of Brabant 1415

PHILIP count of Nevers 1415

LOUIS duke of Orleans mur. 1407 = Valentina Visconti

CHARLES VI 1380–1422 = Isabeau of Bavaria d. 1435

CHARLES duke of Orleans d. 1465 →

Maire of Anjou

John, count of Dunois (illeg.)

ISABELLA d. 1409 = RICHARD II King of England 1377–1399

LOUIS Dauphin d. 1415

JOHN Dauphin d. 1417

KATHERINE d. 1437 = HENRY V King of England 1413–1422

CHARLES VII 1422–1461

LOUIS XI 1461–1483

MARGARET = (1) Louis Dauphin d. 1415 = (2) ARTHUR count of Richemont

Margaret of Bavaria

PHILIP The Good duke of Burgundy d. 1467 = (3) Isabella of Portugal

ANNE d. 1432 = JOHN duke of Bedford d. 1435

CHARLES The Bold duke of Burgundy d. 1477 →

nor could they transmit a claim. Succession had to be entirely through the male line. The rightful heir had to be Philip of Valois, the deceased king's cousin, who had acted as regent whilst awaiting the birth of Charles IV's posthumous child.

The *Grandes Chroniques de France* tell us that an English delegation did come to Paris in 1328 to argue that Edward III, as nephew, was the nearer relative of Charles than Philip as cousin. Some French lawyers may even have agreed, but there was counter argument that Edward's claim was weakened both because it came through a woman and because of his status as a French vassal. The matter was effectively closed by Philip's crowning at the traditional French coronation place of Reims on 29 May 1328.

> It was also argued that it had never been known and envisaged that the kingdom of France should be submitted to the government of the king of England, and that the latter was a vassal and liege man of the king of France. *(Grandes Chroniques de France, on the accession of Philip VI)*

It is difficult to know how seriously the English took the matter of the claim to the French throne in 1328. No effort seems to have been made at that point to use it to negotiate better terms over Gascony. What we can be certain about, however, is that the year 1328 was momentous for both countries. Each had a new king whose title to the throne was unusual, although not suspect. The outbreak of the Hundred Years War is linked to how Philip VI and Edward III tried to assert their authority at home and abroad in the decade that followed.

WARRING SIDES
The English and French monarchies on the eve of the Hundred Years War

Edward III and Philip VI

Although both kings were secure on their thrones, their mode of accession – Philip by the choice of the magnates, and Edward's by the deposition of his father – created some weaknesses. The English monarchy remained weaker for longer, during which time the advantage lay with the French. At the point of their accessions, Edward was only 14, Philip 35.

Philip's position was fortified by an early military victory. The Count of Flanders, Louis of Nevers, took refuge at the French court in 1325 in the face of rebellion led by Bruges. At Philip's coronation, Louis again asked for aid. At first, Philip and his magnates were reluctant to act, mindful of the disaster of Courtrai in 1302 when the flower of French chivalry had been defeated by the Flemish infantry, but by the end of July 1328 an army had been arrayed. On 23 August Philip led his men to a cavalry-based victory against the Flemish at Cassel (half-way between St-Omer and Ypres), and Louis was restored. The matter of Flanders persisted, however, for Louis was driven out again in 1339, leaving the way open for Edward to ally with the Flemish townsmen. This led directly to Edward's assumption of the title 'King of France' at Ghent in January 1340. Louis' loyalty to Philip led to his own death at Crécy.

His confidence boosted, Philip took an aggressive stance against England, prompted by the long-standing issues of vassalage as well as by an implicit desire to neutralize Edward's potential claim to the French throne. If Edward could be forced to pay homage for his French lands, he would thereby recognize Philip as king. Edward would be very vulnerable if he refused, especially after an assembly of French nobility told Philip that he could sequestrate the revenues of Gascony and Ponthieu if Edward defaulted. Edward thus paid homage in Amiens Cathedral on 6 June 1329, fearing loss of money or, worse, an invasion of his French lands. Philip had been planning an army of 5,000 men-at-arms and 16,000 infantry in the early months of 1329; the English had responded by making plans of their own, although by no means on the same scale. Whether these preparations were more than mere posturing is difficult to tell.

Edward deliberately limited in scope the homage which he paid to Philip VI in June 1329 in an effort to keep his options open. Whilst this had averted a possible conflict, it led to further pressure from Philip in May 1330, to which Edward had little choice but to succumb in order to keep his lands and revenues in France. Although from October 1330 Edward was fully in control of his own government, he could not afford a war with France. Thus on 30 March 1331 he accepted that his homage of 1329 should have been liege, though he did not attend another ceremony.

I become your man for the duchy of Aquitaine and its appurtenances that I hold of you as duke and peer of France, according to the peace treaty made in the past … and then the hands of the King of England were put between those of the King of France and the kiss was given by the King of France to the King of England. This was done at Amiens in the choir of the cathedral on 6 June 1329. *(Homage of Edward III, from a contemporary text)*

Problems raised by the English king's tenure of lands in France could have led to conflict at any time. The French

had already shown their aggression, but the English were hardly likely to give up the lands without a fight. Significantly, Edward III chose to reappoint as seneschal Sir Oliver Ingham, whose actions against the *bastide* at Saint Sardos had led to war in 1324 and whose removal from office had been required by the French. Ingham proved key to the preservation of the English position

Edward III, King of England, paid homage to Philip VI, King of France, for his lands in France in June 1329, as portrayed in a 15th-century version of the *Grandes Chroniques de France*. (Photo by Photo Josse/ Leemage/Corbis via Getty Images)

in Gascony, especially when war broke out in 1337. But for Edward himself, Scotland was a more pressing issue in the 1330s.

The death of Robert I of Scotland on 7 June 1329 left his five-year-old son, David II, on the throne. In 1332, Edward Balliol, son of the John who had been made king in 1291, chanced his arm with an invasion of Scotland.

Edward of Woodstock, Prince of Wales, later known as the Black Prince, portrayed here on his fine tomb in Canterbury Cathedral, was one of the most renowned military figures of his age, victor of the battles of Poitiers and Nájera. (Photo by RDImages/Epics/Getty Images)

This may have received tacit support from Edward III. Balliol's victory at Dupplin Moor on 11 August 1332 and his subsequent crowning on 26 September encouraged Edward to offer assistance. This he did by coming north with an army, defeating David II's army at Halidon Hill on 19 July 1333. In the following May, David took refuge in France. English armies operated in Scotland into the mid-1330s, with Edward campaigning there in person on several occasions up to July 1336.

The Franco-Scottish alliance, confirmed as recently as 1326, ensured Philip's interest in the matter. More significantly, it enabled Philip in 1334 to introduce a new demand into negotiations on the tenure of Gascony, namely that Scotland should be included in any

diplomatic settlement. This threatened to undermine Edward's freedom of action in Scotland, a move hardly likely to be pleasing to him when he now had a chance of reversing the defeats of earlier decades against his northern neighbours. Philip's demand was tantamount not only to preventing any advance in negotiations over outstanding problems in Gascony, but also to preventing a settlement over Scotland. A further complication here was Philip's intention to launch a crusade to the Holy Land.

Military organization

It is at this point that we need to review the military potential of both sides. Both had recent experience of war, and thus the raising of armies was well established. In France, the king deployed his feudal rights to summon the nobility to service and to call out the population through the *arrière-ban*. In practice, the latter was often used to raise money in lieu of service. In England, these rights were less formal, but the king was able to rely on the military support of the nobility and of the shire levies. In both countries, all soldiers were remunerated with pay, such developments having begun in the reigns of Edward I and Philip IV.

There was ample armed might at the kings' disposal, although it had to be called out on each occasion and needed time to assemble. Thus response time was slow. No one doubted the king's right to wage war. All wars were portrayed as defensive, fought in defence of the rights of the ruler, but they were already wars of the king *and* his people, because the king was the defender of his subjects. His rights were their rights. This could easily be fanned by propaganda in which the churches of both countries assisted with orders for prayers for the king's endeavours. The church was already a source of royal taxation in both countries, the controversy over that issue being won by both kings in the face of wars from 1290 to 1310.

The potential for larger armies (around 20,000) lay with the French because their country had a higher population. Records of a hearth tax (*fouage*) levied in 1328 suggest a total population of 12.25 million. England is unlikely to have had more than six million. Although France contained many semi-independent provinces, this made little difference (save in civil war) to the king's ability to raise men from a wide geographical area as troops were recruited through the nobility of the areas, as well as through towns under royal control. Actions would often see troops drawn from neighbouring locations. Thus Languedoc provided men for campaigns in Gascony, whereas troops from north of the Loire would be used in the northern theatre.

The English were at a disadvantage in that they had to bring troops over the sea. In their lands in the south-west of France, this problem was partly mitigated by the use of

Gascons in their own defence, something that the large number of petty nobility in the area facilitated. Between 4,000 and 7,000 men could be raised in this way. They were pleased to serve for pay, and in defence of their land. For them, better a distant ruler in England than a French king nearer to hand. Moreover, Anglo-Gascon interests were brought closer through economic ties, not least the wine trade. There was some danger of defections to the French. Particularly significant here were the larger tenants and neighbours of the king-duke, such as the Foix, Albret and Armagnac.

If the defence of the duchy needed to be boosted in the face of a major French onslaught, or if campaigns were to be launched outside Gascony, then support from England was needed. Even then, the co-operation of the Gascons was a military advantage in both defence and offence, the latter being well evidenced by their role in the Black Prince's *chevauchées* of 1355 and 1356. The English position was also helped by the rocky terrain and long frontier of their lands in south-west France. Many small fortifications held up any invading army, although places often changed hands with alarming frequency. This generated a war that tied up troops and prevented decisive outcomes. No major pitched battles occurred in Gascony until Castillon in 1453, and no king of either side ever campaigned there.

For campaigns in the north of France, the English did not have local support as they did in Gascony. Ponthieu provided no parallel in terms of troops, and was an area vulnerable to attack, being surrounded by French territory and close to Paris. If the English were to make any impact, Edward III would have to have recourse to the policies pursued by Edward I and John, namely the purchase of alliances with rulers in the Low Countries and Germany for troops. This cost money, and also ran the risk of allies pursuing their own interests. However, without the continental alliances Edward III acquired in the late 1330s (which brought 6,200 men at least), it is doubtful that he could have maintained a large military presence against Philip in the north. It is

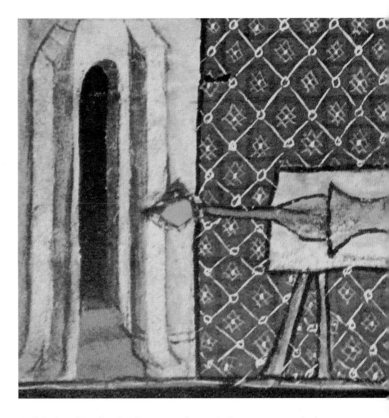

unlikely that he had more than 4,600 men with him from England in 1339. Not until the mid-1340s were systems in England amended to allow the English to field larger armies of their own. Although the military support of allies remained important throughout the whole of the Hundred Years War, it was perhaps never again as significant as it was at the outset.

Arms and armour

In terms of armaments, there was probably little to choose between the English and the French. Already by the beginning of the war, the men-at-arms would have worn plate armour, although its quality improved over the course of the war. Infantry relied more on brigandines – cloth or leather armour reinforced with metal strips,

The treatise on kingship written in 1326 for the young prince Edward includes one of the earliest known illustrations of a gunpowder weapon. (CPA Media Pte Ltd / Alamy Stock Photo)

such strips being cheaper to mass produce and easier to replace than full plate. The French did use the longbow but preferred the crossbow because it had an intrinsically longer range. Being essentially mechanical rather than dependent on man-strength, it was easier to shoot and required less training. It was thus a common weapon of the urban militias. The longbow was cheaper to manufacture, as were its arrows, since crossbow bolts had to be heavier and contain more metal. The real advantage of the longbow was that it could issue ten shots for the crossbow's two. When there were large numbers of archers *en masse*, the longbow was a lethal weapon.

At the beginning of the war, gunpowder weapons were scarce and unsophisticated. They did exist, as manuscript illustrations show, and were used at Sluys and in other engagements, but they were not deployed in larger

The battle of Sluys, called in French L'Ecluse, was a naval victory for the English fought on 24 June 1340, and is illustrated here in a late 15th-century copy of Froissart's *Chroniques*. (Photo by Fine Art Images/ Heritage Images via Getty Images)

quantities until the last quarter of the century, when wrought- and cast-iron pieces could be manufactured. This helps explain why the 14th-century war was largely a series of *chevauchées* and of long and abortive sieges, whereas after 1400, often shorter, successful sieges predominated since fortifications took time to be modified against gunpowder weapons. Both before and after 1400, other kinds of siege engine were used, various throwing devices, as well as large artillery crossbows or *espringalds*, the latter also being used in defence of fortifications. Whilst English towns were not well protected by walls at this point, their French counterparts generally were.

Fighting on home soil and with intrinsically larger manpower potential, the French had the natural advantage. This was also the case with naval forces.

The French kings had their own navy as well as access to Genoese galleys. The English kings were still over-reliant on the requisitioning of merchant vessels that were then provided with defensive structures and fighting platforms. Thus at the beginning of the war, English coasts and shipping were very vulnerable, and this situation was only resolved by Edward's victory at Sluys in June 1340. Ships often contained large numbers of troops, reminding us that hand-to-hand fighting was common, for the aim was to capture ships. They were too scarce and valuable a resource to destroy. Besides, until gunpowder weapons developed there was no easy way of knocking a ship out of action from a distance.

Money

The French king had the advantage in that he could finance his armies mainly from his lands, which brought in 26 tonnes of silver per annum. In the reign of Philip IV there had developed the notion of the king's right, without the need for consultation of any representative assembly, to levy tax for defence, based upon men paying for exemption from military service, but there were many exemptions, not least that of the nobility.

The English king was dependent upon taxation to boost his landed income, which lay at only five tonnes of pure silver per annum. Taxes on moveable property (the lay subsidy) had begun in earnest under Edward I and become virtually annual under Edward II, but needed the consent of the Commons in Parliament. This was not necessarily a weakening factor, for it enabled the king to publicize his intentions and galvanize the nation behind his endeavours. As the English nobility was smaller than that of France, the crown needed to recruit more broadly. This had already been seen in the Scottish wars, where large numbers of Welsh and English archers and foot soldiers were found, and were to be found again in the 1340s. But the armies with which Edward began the war in northern France were largely made up of nobles and their 'mixed retinues' of men-at-arms and archers, usually

The noble was a gold coin struck at the order of Edward III in the mid-1340s. In this example from c. 1350 the king is portrayed standing within a ship, probably recalling his victory at Sluys. (Photo by Heritage Art/Heritage Images via Getty Images)

in a ratio of 1:1. When the English king campaigned in person, troops served for as long as he dictated. If others led his forces, then the system of indenture (contract) was increasingly used whereby conditions and duration of service could be agreed in advance. Edward III relied very much on loans, as his grandfather had done. An important form of security was the English wool export on which finances depended in the early stages of the war. The French king was less well provided with credit systems. In 1335–36 Philip had to rely on revaluations of coinage. Shortage of money contributed to making the large royal-led campaigns short and sporadic.

The proving grounds

Recent military experience was significant. Philip had won a victory at Cassel in 1328, and was intending to crusade in the Levant. Thus he was gathering men, money and ships, as well as generating in his own mind and in the minds of his people an emphasis on military endeavour. Meanwhile, Scotland was providing Edward III's proving ground. He had experienced the difficulties of containing a raiding force in Weardale in 1327. In 1333 he had besieged Berwick, and won a victory in battle at Halidon Hill with an army of perhaps 10,000–13,000. Similarities exist between Edward's tactics at Halidon Hill and at Crécy, not least in the use of arrow fire to impede the enemy advance, although this was then followed up by a cavalry pursuit of the fleeing Scots. The victory at Halidon showed that the English could win, although the Scots were a less formidable and numerous enemy than the French in the context of a pitched battle. Clifford Rogers suggests that Edward's sweeping campaigns into Scotland between 1334 and 1336 were a precursor of his *chevauchées* in France,

intended to show his military might and to bring war 'cruel and sharp' to the people who resisted his authority.

> Each division of the English army had two wings of fine archers. When the armies came into contact they fired their arrows as thickly as the rays of the sun, striking the Scots so that they fell in their thousands and they started to flee from the English in fear of their lives. *(Brut Chronicle on the battle of Halidon Hill)*

It must not be forgotten, however, that Edward had not won his war against the Scots. He was obliged to keep some kind of military presence there even whilst fighting in France. There was always the fear of Scottish raids into England and of French aid to the Scots. The campaigns in Scotland kept the English military machine well oiled; many of those who served Edward there were to do so in France. Whilst an observer in the late 1330s might have given the French the edge in any impending Anglo-French conflict, outcomes of wars were never predictable. At base, neither side had the military capacity to defeat the other in a way that would bring a definitive victory and settlement. In this respect, therefore, the war that broke out in 1337 was already likely to last a long time and to contain many stalemates.

The Luttrell Psalter, commissioned by Sir Geoffrey Luttrell around the beginning of the Hundred Years War, includes marginal illustrations of the famous English longbowmen. (© British Library Board. All Rights Reserved / Bridgeman Images)

OUTBREAK

Mounting tensions: 1336–37

Arguably, had Philip been able to fulfil his crusading plans in 1336, Anglo-French conflict might have been averted, although it is likely that conflict over Gascony would have occurred at some point. Whether it would have arisen over Scotland is more problematic, as the French had been prone to promise military aid to the Scots but not to deliver. It seems unlikely that Edward would have gone to war over his claim to the French crown: he had already gone too far in accepting Philip's kingship. The promoting of the claim as an apparent war aim arose as a *result* of the outbreak of the Hundred Years War, not as its *cause*. Not until 1340 did Edward formally declare himself King of France. War had already broken out in 1337 over Gascony.

An important turning point came in March 1336 when Pope Benedict XII informed Philip that his crusade could not go ahead because the problems of Gascony and Scotland had not been reconciled. 'French resources were liberated for aggressive ventures elsewhere', as Jonathan Sumption puts it. In the summer of 1336, the fleet that Philip had been gathering in Marseilles was diverted to the Channel. The Scots had approached Philip for aid, and he was now thinking of sending an army there. Edward planned a short raid into Scotland in May but was afraid of doing more. A council held at Northampton on 25 June advised the sending of an embassy to France, but this did nothing to divert the French.

Edward had most to fear at this stage, faced as he was with three possible theatres – Gascony, Scotland and perhaps England itself. As it happened, Philip did not send aid to the Scots. Although Edward began to organize another campaign to Scotland, this was cancelled in November 1336. Thenceforward Edward relied on Balliol and a few English troops left for the latter's assistance. It is easy to dismiss fears of a French invasion of England in the light of hindsight, given that we know Philip never did launch a major assault. But the English government found it a useful propaganda ploy at the time of the Crécy expedition in 1346 to claim that he had so intended, sending back to England from Caen a document that purported to show the details of his plans for a landing in 1336 of 20,000 men, largely Normans, who were the maritime rivals of the southern English.

French ships carried out raids on Orford and on the Isle of Wight in the late summer of 1336, and there was plenty of panic. At a council held at Nottingham on 24 September, an array of troops for defence of the coasts was ordered. This is the point at which, to quote Sumption again, 'the English political community accepted that war with France was inevitable'. Increasingly, both nations were put on a war footing, with orders for the requisitioning of ships, the raising of loans, and the seizing of the goods of alien merchants.

Philip was already planning in late 1336 how he might invade Gascony, coming to an agreement with the Count of Foix for the service of 600 men for two months. At the same time, Edward sought allies amongst France's northern neighbours. Already he was considering possible action against Philip in northern France, either in person or through the military aid of such allies, which was crucial to him in terms of manpower. Philip's envoys were equally busy at this point in acquiring allies and limiting support for Edward.

There can be no doubt that Philip provoked the opening of actual war. In December 1336, he ordered

Edward to hand over Robert of Artois, Philip's brother-in-law, who had fled from France under charges of murder. Robert's presence in England had already been a further factor in souring Anglo-French relations between 1334 and 1336. The order to surrender Robert was delivered not to Edward in England, but to Ingham as seneschal in Aquitaine. Philip's legal authority over Edward only functioned where the latter was duke. But Artois was in England not Gascony, and it was legally problematic whether an action by the king-duke in England was within the remit of the French king. Indeed, the matter points again to the underlying problem – the tenure of lands in one kingdom by the king of another. How much influence Robert of Artois had over Edward's strategy is unclear, but some have suggested that it was he who heightened the king's awareness of the potential value of a claim to the French throne.

Arguably, Edward could have averted war by surrendering Robert. Since he did not choose to do so, we must conclude that he was willing to engage in conflict. Although in the spring of 1337 another embassy was sent to France, Edward was now making formal preparations for war. This is particularly noticeable at the Parliament of March 1337 where six new earls were created, with a view to creating a cadre of military commanders. Edward still considered that armies might be needed for Scotland as well as Gascony. He may at first have intended to go to Gascony in person, but by early July he had changed his mind. It seems likely that his change of plan was caused by what he had learned of Philip's intentions.

When Philip issued the *arrière-ban* on 30 April 1337, two theatres of action became obvious, for the French armies were ordered to assemble by 8 July at Amiens as well as at Marmande on the frontier of Edward's duchy, only 50 miles (80km) from Bordeaux. A few hundred troops were sent from England to Gascony in late August. Edward took the chance that he could rely on the Gascons to maintain their own defence, under the guidance of his officials and their retinues in the duchy. Edward was now intending to join his Low Country

The close relationship between Philip VI and Robert of Artois was undermined by a dispute over the inheritance of the county of Artois, which led to Robert supporting Edward III. (Photo by: Christophel Fine Art/Universal Images Group via Getty Images)

allies for a campaign against Philip in the north, but for various reasons he did not cross to Brabant until 16 July 1338. By this time, fighting in Gascony was well under way and serious raids on England had commenced.

It is not easy to define the first action of the Hundred Years War. There was no 'declaration of war' in the modern sense. As we saw, there were some French raids in 1336, and the Scottish theatre was in some ways already a war between England and France. But perhaps we might take the opening action as the failed attempt of one of Philip's officials to seize Saint Macaire in February 1337. Once Philip declared the *arrière-ban* on 30 April there was no turning back: he had given clear indication of his intentions to wage war on a large and national scale. The legal niceties were still to be performed. On 24 May, after Philip's council had endorsed his decision to declare confiscate Edward III's lands in France, the *bailli* of

The great seal of Edward III after the treaty of Brétigny of 1360, which gives Edward's title as King of England and Lord of Ireland and Aquitaine. (duncan1890/Getty Images)

Great Seal of Edward III.

Amiens was instructed to take possession of Ponthieu. By 13 June Philip's letters declaring Aquitaine forfeit had been delivered to Edward's seneschal in the duchy, and within a few weeks French troops were launching their invasion.

The Hundred Years War thus effectively began, as it was to end, in Gascony. It seems thus far to be following the pattern of the wars fought in 1294 and 1324. So far, too, Edward III had done no more than express his desire to defend his possessions in France and his perceived rights in Scotland. In August 1337, a manifesto was distributed to various magnates and royal officials who were to explain the king's business to meetings ordered to be held in the shires. Here Edward's reasons for the war were clearly stated: the French king had offered assistance to the Scots and usurped Edward's rights in Gascony, and had maliciously accused the latter of hindering the crusade. Significantly, there was no mention of a claim to the French crown.

> [Philip] striving by all means that he could to undo the King of England and his people, so that he could keep what he had wrongfully withheld and conquer more from him, refused all offers, but, seeking his opportunities, busied himself in aid and maintenance of the Scots, the enemies of the King of England, attempting to delay him by the Scottish war so that he would have no power to pursue his rights elsewhere. *(Edward's manifesto of August 1337, from the Close Rolls)*

THE FIGHTING

The Hundred Years War: a narrative

The first phase: 1337–60

Given the length and complexity of the war, it is possible here to concentrate only on direct Anglo-French conflict. It must be remembered, however, that fighting also took place in Scotland, the Low Countries and Spain, and that troops from many areas were involved. In this respect, as in the diplomatic context, it is fair to see the Hundred Years War as the first pan-European war.

It began, like the wars of 1294 and 1324, in Aquitaine. In July 1337 the French army, which launched its attack through the Agenais, and the Count of Foix's force, which entered from the south, pursued campaigns of harassment and small-scale devastation. This is a timely reminder that the French were often as keen on the *chevauchée*-style raid as the English. This strategy was preferred when troops were few and money inadequate for long-term operations and occupation, and when war was intended to be waged on more than one front.

In 1338, the French launched further attacks through the Agenais and Saintonge. Although these were repulsed by the seneschal and his Gascon supporters, the lack of reinforcements from England meant that by the spring of 1339 the French were able to make serious inroads and were now establishing garrisons along the Dordogne and Garonne. Bordeaux was threatened with encirclement

A *pavillon d'or* of Philip VI issued in 1339 which portrays the crowned king on a throne under a canopy. Philip's sceptre is topped by the fleur-de-lys. (Photo by Heritage Art/Heritage Images via Getty Images)

after the key outposts of Bourg and Blaye fell with the assistance of a French fleet in April 1339.

Philip intended to keep an army of 12,000 on the Garonne only until June 1339, at which point he planned to concentrate all his forces along the Somme in anticipation of the invasion of Edward and his allies. But Edward's delayed arrival led to French pressure on Gascony continuing. Siege was now laid to Bordeaux itself, but the attackers' supplies were low and they departed after only a week. Ingham was able to carry out some raids towards Toulouse in October, perhaps even intended as a co-ordinated move with Edward's invasion in the north.

The delay in Edward's crossing facilitated a number of damaging hit-and-run raids by the French on the south-coast ports. An attack on Portsmouth on 24 March 1338 was followed immediately by an attack on Jersey. The French took control of Guernsey on 8 September 1338 and held it for a few years. Although the English tried to raise a fleet against such incursions, the French were able to launch a serious attack on Southampton on Sunday, 5 October 1338.

In 1339 there were fears that Philip was planning a major assault on England from Normandy. The raid, when it came in May, was less sustained than expected, but enough to harry the coasts of Devon, Sussex and Kent. Only in July had the English gathered enough ships together to counter a planned attack on the Cinque ports. Had it not been for a mutiny of Philip's Genoese seamen, the position of England could have been much more precarious. In August the English began to take the war to the French with a raid on Le Tréport, but this was too little, too late. The French had already recognized the importance of taking the war to the English, and of creating uncertainty on the coasts and in the sea lanes.

In both Gascony and the Channel, therefore, the English were losing the war in its first stages.

The war in the north: 1337–39

Over the summer of 1337 Edward brokered deals with Low Country rulers for military aid, being promised almost 7,000 men, including 2,000 from the Emperor, Lewis IV, of Bavaria, for two months. These agreements served to limit Edward's freedom of action in terms of where the war should be fought. His own plan may have been to invade Normandy, with the other princes attacking France from the north-east, but the negotiations had led to an agreement that the coalition would operate together from Hainault into the Cambrésis. This served the interests of the princes and especially the emperor, under whose theoretical imperial authority Cambrai lay. But Edward was distracted by problems in Scotland, and the assembly with his allies, initially intended for September 1337, was postponed and finally abandoned in late November. A few English troops crossed under Walter de Mauny, carrying out hit-and-run raids on the Flemish coast.

That there was a lull in hostilities after this point was due to the attempted mediation of cardinals over the winter months, which led Edward to promise to refrain from an attack on France until March 1338. Nonetheless, the basic strategy of the coalition was preserved and formed the basis of the campaigns of 1338. By the end of February, Edward was raising his army of 4,500, finally crossing to Antwerp in the duchy of Brabant on 16 July 1338. This landing led Philip to order his own army to assemble on the northern frontier, with Philip himself arriving at Amiens on 24 August. But no military action ensued because Edward found his allies reluctant to fight without receipt of pay and without the presence of the emperor.

Edward travelled to meet Lewis of Bavaria on 5 September at Koblenz and was given the title 'vicar general of the Empire', being authorized to act 'throughout Germany and France and all the provinces and parts thereof'. Edward was now able to finalize the campaign into the Cambrésis, although the initial start date was again postponed to July 1339 as he tried to organise his finances.

Philip intended to be ready for the invasion. He placed 6,000 troops in garrisons along the border with Hainault over the winter of 1338–39, and planned to combine his military might, which was potentially as high as 50,000, by moving troops from the Gascon theatre to the Somme in the summer of 1339. The French nobility received their summons to be at Compiègne by 22 July 1339, but as Edward's invasion had still not occurred, the assembly

In seeking the support of Emperor Lewis of Bavaria, who is depicted here, Edward travelled to Koblenz and accepted the title of 'vicar general of the Empire'. (imageBROKER / Alamy Stock Photo)

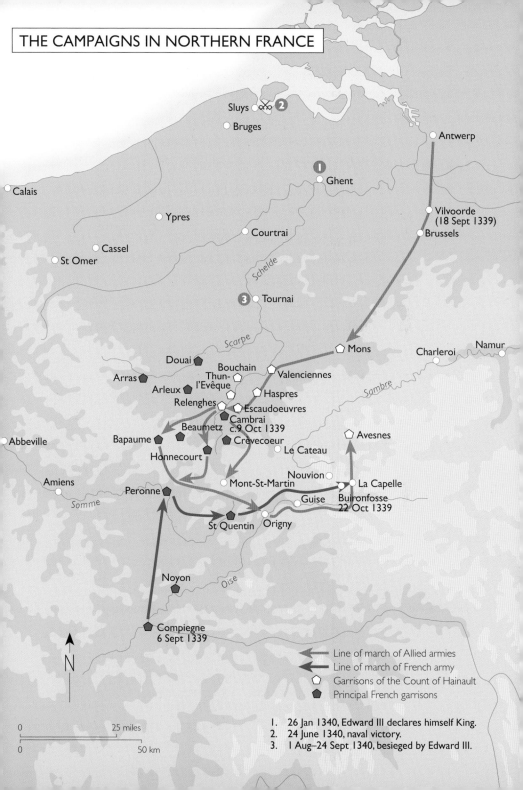

THE CAMPAIGNS IN NORTHERN FRANCE

Sluys ⚔ ❷
Bruges

Antwerp

Calais

❶
Ghent

Ypres

Vilvoorde
(18 Sept 1339)
Brussels

Courtrai

Cassel

St Omer

Schelde

❸ Tournai

Mons   Charleroi   Namur

Scarpe

Douai
Bouchain
Thun-   Valenciennes
l'Evêque
Arras
Arleux   *Sambre*
Relenghes   Haspres
Escaudoeuvres
Cambrai   Avesnes
Beaumetz   c.9 Oct 1339
Bapaume   Crèvecoeur
Honnecourt   Le Cateau

Abbeville

Amiens   Nouvion
Mont-St-Martin   La Capelle
Peronne   Guise   Buironfosse
                                               22 Oct 1339
Somme   St Quentin   Origny

Noyon

Oise

Compiegne
6 Sept 1339

N

←— Line of march of Allied armies
←— Line of march of French army
⬠ Garrisons of the Count of Hainault
⬠ Principal French garrisons

0 _____ 25 miles
0 _____ 50 km

1. 26 Jan 1340, Edward III declares himself King.
2. 24 June 1340, naval victory.
3. 1 Aug–24 Sept 1340, besieged by Edward III.

was postponed to 6 September. Meanwhile, Edward and his allies began to assemble at Vilvoorde, beginning their march forward to Valenciennes on 18 September 1339. Exactly a week earlier, Philip had taken the symbolic banner known as the Oriflamme from Saint Denis. This was, in effect, the real opening of full war between the two kings.

> Forth he fared into France … and all his company. The noble Duke of Brabant went with him into that land, ready to live or die. Then the rich fleur de lis won there little glory. Fast he fled in fear. The rightful heir of that country came with all his knights to shake him by the beard. *(The English poet Laurence Minot on the expedition into the Cambrésis)*

Edward and his allies, with an army numbering 10,000–15,000, entered the Cambrésis, where Edward had authority by virtue of his imperial vicariate. It was no doubt deliberate that they crossed into France on 9 October, the festival of St Denis. They had few supplies with them, implying that they thought that Philip would be drawn to battle quickly. Their need to live off the land prompted considerable pillaging – a useful way, too, of undermining Philip's reputation as a defender of his people. A papal alms-giving exercise in the following year reveals that 45 villages suffered damage. Never before had French civilians been victims of war on such a scale.

The French probably intended to give battle on 14 October, but Edward was not ready and withdrew eastwards over the Oise. A formal challenge was sent by the French for battle on 21 or 22 October. Edward accepted this, and chose his position at Buironfosse. He drew up his army in a formation reminiscent of Halidon Hill, with archers on the flanks and the customary three battles in the centre. Many were knighted by Edward, indicating that he believed battle would be given.

There is still controversy over which side decided against engagement. Sumption suggests that Philip decided to dig in to force Edward to attack at a disadvantage, but the latter refused as he was outnumbered two to one, and the French were protected by trenches. Rogers, however, suggests that it was Philip who withdrew on the advice of his council, who explained that 'if he were defeated he would lose his life and his realm, but if the enemy won, he would not have conquered the realm of England nor the lands and possessions of the other lords of England'. The campaign thus ended inconclusively, although arguably the English had shown their strength in being able to cause so much devastation unchecked. But Edward had not claimed the throne at his invasion, justifying it instead through the imperial vicariate.

The campaign of 1340

The campaign of 1340 was more explicitly linked to Edward's claim to the crown. The Flemish townsmen entered the English allegiance, prompted by economic interests and by the desire to have the rebellion against their count legitimized. Thus in Ghent on 26 January 1340, Edward declared himself King of France and henceforward waged war as a putative king of that country. Whether he believed he had any real chance of becoming king is unclear, but the taking up of the title made the war more bitter, and impossible to end without a decisive military event.

Philip's plans were to revenge himself on Hainault and Brabant, and he moved his army towards Cambrai. Edward and his allies chose Tournai just to the north to deflect this French advance, and as a pro-Flemish gesture, since this town had once been in Flemish hands. The plan was for a three-pronged attack by the Flemish militias, the Count of Hainault and other allies, and the English (although Edward himself had returned to England in March). But the French advance was not prevented, and there was further devastation caused by the French towards Cambrai.

The situation again looked unpromising for the English, but there were two areas of success. In Gascony, the Lord of Albret decided to throw his lot in with the English, which placed the French in the Agenais on the

defensive. But more significant was success at sea. Philip raised a fleet of over 200 vessels aimed at intercepting Edward when he returned with 2,000 men in June 1340. But it was instead the English fleet that caught the French in the estuary of the Zwin at Sluys on 24 June 1340. This was a complete disaster for the French, with 90 per cent of their ships being captured, and high losses of men, perhaps as high as 18,000.

This enabled Edward to resume the plan to besiege Tournai, with another army being sent into Artois under Robert of Artois. But the expedition met with disaster at St-Omer, thus weakening Edward's chances at Tournai, which he had invested on 1 August, by exposing him to the French army. The French drew up at Bouvines, site of their victory against King John in 1214. But again Philip seems to have been reluctant to engage. Through the mediation of Jeanne, the dowager Countess of Hainault, sister of Philip VI and mother-in-law of Edward, a truce was agreed on 24 September for nine months.

The opening of the theatre in Brittany

After the expiry of the truce, the balance of control in Aquitaine fell to the French, who placed 12,500 men in garrisons, but in the autumn of 1342 Ingham launched an invasion of Saintonge. It was proving difficult for either side to hold conquests for long. This unstable situation, with almost continuous military action, also encouraged the growth of informal war. Already *routiers* were as active in French- as in English-held lands.

In the meantime, Edward planned an invasion for 1341 with 13,500 troops, of which two-thirds would be archers, the first sign that he felt that he needed to boost his infantry. He intended another northern campaign but his allies were lukewarm and preferred to extend the truce to June 1342. Thus over the winter of 1341–42 Edward turned his attention to Scotland, not least because David II had returned with French assistance in June 1341.

Into this scenario a new element emerged, the disputed succession of Brittany. Duke John III, who

OPPOSITE
Jacob van Artevelde was instrumental in the acceptance of Edward III as King of France by the towns of Ghent, Bruges and Ypres. This monument in the Vrijdagmarkt, Ghent was erected in 1863. (santirf/Getty Images)

A *gros* of Charles de Blois, the French-supported claimant to the duchy of Brittany, who was killed at the battle of Auray in 1364. (YA/BOT / Alamy Stock Photo)

had served in Philip's army at Tournai, died on 30 April 1341. The dead duke's half-brother, John de Montfort, acted decisively in seizing the main towns. Philip was reluctant to allow him the duchy, being moved by his preference for the rival claimant, the late duke's nephew-in-law, Charles de Blois, and by suspicions, which were well founded, that de Montfort had already been in secret discussions with Edward. Philip acted swiftly to recover Nantes and most of eastern Brittany, and imprisoned de Montfort in Paris before Edward decided in mid-February 1342 in favour of a campaign. Brittany then became the main focus of English military efforts, with Scotland being largely abandoned.

An advance force of 234 men was despatched under de Mauny in May, and a force of 1,350 under the Earl of Northampton in August. The latter, dug in around Morlaix, defeated an attack by Charles de Blois on 30 September 1342, which perhaps should have the credit of being the first real battle of the Hundred Years War, although fought on a small scale and with no specific gain for the English.

Edward III himself landed in Brittany on 26 October with 5,000 men. That the king had chosen to campaign here in person is significant. The most important theatre was bound to be where the king himself was. The main focus was a siege laid to Vannes, but raiding parties were also sent out. There was chance of a battle when Philip's son John, Duke of Normandy, advanced towards Vannes in January 1343, but the French drew off.

Edward's campaign proved inconclusive because reinforcements from England were not forthcoming. So a further truce was agreed from 19 January 1343 to 29 September 1346 to facilitate negotiations under papal authority at Avignon. Brittany remained divided, encouraging a war of attrition for many years: the north and east lay under de Blois and the French, and the south and west under the Montfortians and the English.

The campaigns of 1345–47

Edward repudiated the truce in the summer of 1345, buoyed up by the homage not only of John de Montfort, who had escaped from France, but also of a renegade Norman noble, Godfrey de Harcourt. Plans were made for armies to advance to Brittany, to Gascony under Henry of Grosmont (later Duke of Lancaster), and to northern France under the king. The latter did not proceed because of uncertainty of the Flemish alliance. In Brittany there was less success as sieges of Quimper (where John de Montfort died on 26 September) and Guingcamp failed, but in the following June, Charles de Blois was defeated by Sir Thomas Dagworth at Saint-Pol de Léon.

The Gascon campaign, with 2,000 men from England and several thousand locally raised men, was the first major English military effort in the duchy and led to the recapture of the important town of Bergerac. The French in their turn besieged Auberoche, but were attacked by Henry, Earl of Derby and defeated on 21 October 1345. This severely undermined their attack and led to the English re-occupation of La Réole as well as penetration into the Agenais by the capture of Aiguillon and elsewhere in the early months of 1346. This was serious enough to merit the laying of siege to Aiguillon in April 1346 by the Duke of Normandy (later John II).

The position of the English was now much stronger than at any previous point in the war. The year 1346 was an important turning point not only in Edward's level of success on all fronts, but also in the kind of preparations he made for his own campaign. Gone was the reliance on allies. Now the focus was on independent action against

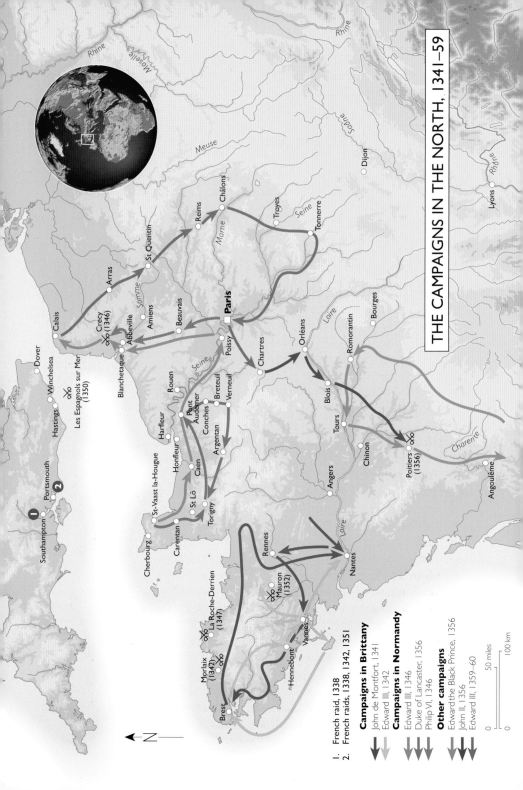

THE CAMPAIGNS IN THE NORTH, 1341–59

1. French raid, 1338
2. French raids, 1338, 1342, 1351

Campaigns in Brittany
John de Montfort, 1341
Edward III, 1342

Campaigns in Normandy
Edward III, 1346
Duke of Lancaster, 1356
Philip VI, 1346

Other campaigns
Edward the Black Prince, 1356
John II, 1356
Edward III, 1359–60

0   50 miles
0   100 km

N

Rhine
Moselle
Meuse
Saône
Rhine
Marne
Seine
Troyes
Châlons
Reims
Tonnerre
Dijon
Lyons
Rhône
St Quentin
Arras
Amiens
Beauvais
Calais
Crécy (1346)
Abbeville
Blanchetaque
Somme
Paris
Poissy
Chartres
Orléans
Bourges
Romorantin
Loire
Seine
Rouen
Harfleur
Honfleur
Pont Audemer
Breteuil
Verneuil
Conches
Argentan
Caen
St Lô
Torigny
Carentan
St-Vaast la-Hougue
Cherbourg
Dover
Winchelsea
Hastings
Les Espagnols sur Mer (1350)
Portsmouth
Southampton
Blois
Tours
Chinon
Angers
Nantes
Loire
Rennes
Mauron (1352)
Morlaix (1342)
Brest
La Roche-Derrien (1347)
Vannes
Hennebont
Poitiers (1356)
Charente
Angoulême

the French, facilitated by the recruitment of an *English* army that was more securely funded.

A military assessment had been carried out of landowners based on their income. A 100-shilling landowner was to provide an archer, a £10 landowner a *hobelar* (lightly armed mounted soldier), whilst those worth £25 were to provide a man-at-arms. Many of those assessed are known to have served on the campaign of 1346 or at the siege of Calais. Others sent men in their stead, not least the older men who sent their sons. The army was boosted by those serving in return for pardons. Andrew Ayton suggests that the foot soldiers were notably undisciplined, especially at the sacking of Caen, despite Edward's order to the contrary.

It is likely that many Englishmen saw their first service in France in 1346. But how many were there? Despite the existence of a wide range of source materials, the exact number with which Edward landed at Saint-

The castle of Caen, captured briefly by Edward III in 1346. Henry V took the castle again in 1417 and it was not lost by the English until 1450. (Patrick, Flickr, CC BY-SA 2.0)

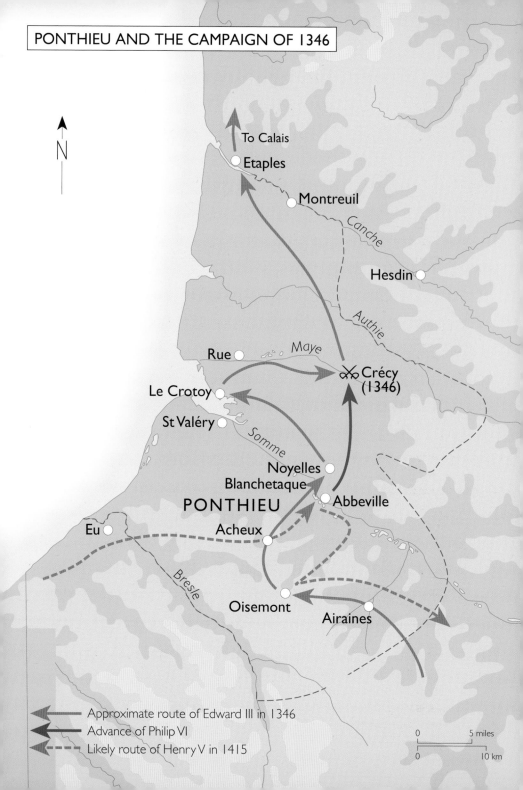

PONTHIEU AND THE CAMPAIGN OF 1346

N

To Calais

Etaples

Montreuil

Canche

Hesdin

Authie

Maye

Rue

Crécy
(1346)

Le Crotoy

St Valéry

Somme

Noyelles

Blanchetaque

PONTHIEU

Abbeville

Eu

Acheux

Bresle

Oisemont

Airaines

Approximate route of Edward III in 1346

Advance of Philip VI

Likely route of Henry V in 1415

0   5 miles

0   10 km

Vaast-La-Hougue on 12 July 1346 remains uncertain. Sumption argues for 7,000–10,000, but Rogers has put the figure at 15,250, comprising 2,700 men-at-arms, 2,300 Welsh spearmen, 7,000 foot English and Welsh archers, and 3,250 mounted archers, *hobelars* and others.

This was a considerable military effort aimed at a frontal attack on Philip. It was Edward's first long and swift march of the war, setting an example that formed the basis of English strategy for the rest of the century. Caen fell to him on 26 July, but his intention was to make a show rather than a conquest: one isolated base in enemy territory would not be practicable. He chose rather to move ever closer to Paris itself, the first time the French crown had been put under real pressure.

Edward certainly intended battle. So too did Philip, but the latter hesitated when it might have fallen more to his advantage – whilst the English were at Poissy close to the capital. Thus the encounter was on 26 August at Crécy within Edward's hereditary land of Ponthieu, and, interestingly, a place that he had visited in the pre-war period. Although the English were outnumbered (the French army numbered around 20,000–25,000), Edward's position was well chosen for both attack and defence, with his archers on the wings, and protection to the rear and sides. The French were thus forced to become over-concentrated in their attack, and to attack uphill.

Philip was impetuous in allowing his Genoese crossbowmen to engage before the rest of his army was arrayed. In fact, there was no need to attack that day, as it was already 5.00pm when the French arrived. His folly led to over 1,500 leading French knights and nobles meeting their death, along with innumerable others of lower rank. This was a major blow not only to French pride but also to their command structures.

French realisation of the level of Edward's threat is witnessed by Philip's order of 20 August for John to abandon the siege of Aiguillon. This opened the gates to further English success in the region, facilitating Lancaster's advance into Saintonge in mid-September, which culminated in the sack of Poitiers (4 October)

where over 600 civilians died. Although the duke did not occupy the area, his action created much insecurity and further encouraged local feuds and guerrilla warfare.

The French defeat prompted a Scottish invasion, which was overcome at Neville's Cross near Durham on 14 October. David II had taken up a position on high ground much as Edward had done at Crécy, but there were in contrast too many hedges and trees to allow him full frontal freedom. David was captured, and not released until 1357.

Edward began to lay siege to Calais from 3 September 1346. Rogers argues that this had been his objective for some time. Calais, unlike Caen, only needed defence on the land side, as it could be protected by sea from England. No longer was Edward willing to rely on his Low Country allies for a regular entry point into France. The siege was a major effort for both sides. Indeed, Rogers suggests that it was the largest single military operation undertaken by the English until the modern period. For Edward, 32,000 man-units were employed until the surrender on 4 August 1347, although the exact numbers there at any one time are not clear. Again these were English troops, around half of them archers, assisted by English ships in blockade. Philip took the Oriflamme on 18 March 1347, and contemplated engaging the besieging army, but he hesitated too long. By July, the English were exceptionally strong, and Philip departed without giving battle. Edward was free to develop Calais as a naval and military base, repopulating it with Englishmen.

A further success arose in Brittany. There Charles de Blois, trying, like David II, to create a diversionary tactic, laid siege to La Roche Derrien in late May 1347, keen to draw Thomas Dagworth to battle. But the plan misfired, and in a hard, hand-to-hand fight, de Blois was captured.

Further military action was threatened but both Edward and Philip were suffering from war exhaustion. Thus a papally mediated truce intervened, and the Black Death prevented further action for a while, although the informal actions in the south-west never abated. In August 1349 the French broke the truce with an invasion of Saintonge and Poitou against English-held fortresses. In December, Lancaster responded with a counter-move down the Garonne into the Agenais and Languedoc towards Toulouse, during which many villages were burned. This may have served as an inspiration for the Black Prince's *chevauchée* of 1355.

OPPOSITE
The English victory at Crécy on 26 August 1346 as portrayed in a late 15th-century version of Froissart's *Chroniques*. (Photo by: Photo12/ Universal Images Group via Getty Images)

The town of Calais commissioned Auguste Rodin in 1884 to create a sculpture in bronze of the Burghers of Calais. This casting is housed in The Metropolitan Museum of Art. (The Metropolitan Museum of Art, New York, Gift of Iris and B. Gerald Cantor, 1989, CC0, www.metmuseum. org)

The campaigns of the 1350s

Philip VI died on 2 August 1350. The new king, John II, carried out military reforms in 1351, ensuring that all men were within companies of between 25 and 80. Previously, discipline and command had been undermined by the tendency of men to move between retinues as it suited them. Fortnightly musters were also introduced. But a cloud was on the horizon with threats that Charles de Navarre, grandson of Louis X, and a large landholder in Normandy, might ally with the English.

The war dragged on rather inconclusively. On 29 August 1350, Edward defeated a Castilian fleet off Winchelsea, although his ramming tactics almost brought disaster. There were many small-scale actions, such as sorties from Calais, and actions in Brittany. The south-west remained on a war footing, with both sides deploying companies a hundred or so strong to effect recovery of places. Such

THE CAMPAIGNS OF EDWARD THE BLACK PRINCE, 1355–56

Edward the Black Prince in Languedoc, Oct–Dec 1355

The Black Prince's march through France, July–Sept 1356

Route of French army, 1356

Duke of Lancaster

BAY OF BISCAY

N

GASCONY

ARMAGNAC

LANGUEDOC

MEDITERRANEAN SEA

0   50 miles

0   100 km

Chartres

Orléans

Châteauneuf

Meung

Gien

Blois

Loire

Angers

Amboise

Romorantin

Cosne

Nantes

Loire

Tours

Saumur

Montbazon

Aubigny

La Charité

Loches

Vierzon

Bourges

Nevers

Châtellerault

La Haye

Issoudun

Decise

Poitiers

Chauvigny

Argenton

St-Benoit

Lussac

Châteauroux

Le Dorat

Bellac

Cartempe

Lesterps

La Peruse

Angoulême

Dronne

Isle

Périgueux

Dordogne

Bordeaux

Libourne

St-Macaire

Bergerac

Langon

Bazas

La Réole

Cahors

Lot

Agen

Aveyron

Labastide d'Armagnac

Monclar

Midouze

Montauban

Tarn

Adour

Albi

Bayonne

Plaisance

Gimont

Toulouse

Montesquiou

Lombez

Aurade

St Lys

Montgiscard

Mirande

Villefranche

Avignonet

Castelnaudary

Capestang

Sauveterre

d'Astarac

Boulbonne

Prouille

Carcassonne

Béziers

Garonne

Limoux

Homps

Narbonne

Foix

Poitiers

Vienne

Creuse

Clain

Indre

Cher

Charente

Gers

Arrats

Baïse

Douzs

actions even occurred during peace negotiations directed by the cardinals. The proposed settlement, that Edward should have full sovereignty in Aquitaine, Poitou and the Limousin, reveals the perceived level of his military success to date rather than acceptance of the seriousness of his claim to the throne.

The French reneged on these negotiations. In response Edward planned another major assault. Lancaster was to lead a force to Normandy in July 1355 to ally with Charles de Navarre. But de Navarre changed his mind, and the expedition was cancelled. Edward's own campaign to Picardy did proceed, bringing in through Calais 5,000 men to join 1,000 allies. But John II's scorched-earth policy forced an early withdrawal, and the Scottish capture of Berwick needed Edward's attention.

An army of 2,200 was despatched under the Black Prince to Bordeaux in September. The intention was to launch, with Gascon aid, a swift raid into Languedoc aimed largely at the lands of the Count of Armagnac. What made this *chevauchée*, which reached almost as far as the Mediterranean, such a success was the level of booty taken and the almost complete lack of risk. There was no French counter-attack, and the prince wisely avoided large fortified centres. The raid did much damage to the local economy, for nothing on this scale had been seen before: Languedoc was an area previously outside the actions of the war.

More importantly, the raid of 1355 emboldened the prince. Over the winter the English took key places as well as booty in raids up the Dordogne. By the summer of 1356 another two-pronged attack had been planned, with Lancaster landing at Saint-Vaast-La-Hougue on 18 June, to join with Charles de Navarre's brother, Philip, and troops from Brittany. An encircling *chevauchée* was conducted through Lower Normandy, with much pillaging. In the meantime, the prince moved off from Bordeaux on 6 July with around 7,000 men, some two-thirds of whom were Gascons. His move towards the Loire was as audacious as that of 1355, but it did not prove possible to make the intended reconnoitre with Lancaster or to cross the Loire.

OPPOSITE
This portrayal of John II, the first known portrait of a French king, has been dated to 1360, the year of his release from imprisonment in England after capture at the battle of Poitiers. (Peter Barritt / Alamy Stock Photo)

Saint-Vaast-La-Hougue, a small port on the eastern side of the Cotentin, was the landing place of Edward III's army in 1346 and of the Duke of Clarence's army in 1412. (Véronique Derouet/Getty Images)

Thus the prince began his return march, but found the French blocking his route at Poitiers. If he did not engage, there would be the danger of an attack on his rear as he moved towards Bordeaux. At first he negotiated for a withdrawal, which the French refused. Then, mindful of his experience at Crécy where he had committed the vanguard, on 19 September he took up a defensive position on a hill, protected in the rear by woodland and by various hazards, including a hedge and marsh in front. Although the English archers again slowed down the French advance, and mowed down the first French battle, equally significant was the feigned retreat of the Earl of Warwick, which drew French troops into the marsh, and the mounted manoeuvre of the Gascon captain, the Captal de Buch, around the rear of the French army. As at Agincourt, it seems that the retreating first battle of the French collided with the second as it advanced. Thus although the French had the numerical superiority with at least 10,000 men, their weight of numbers in a confined space contributed to their undoing.

But the true importance of the battle lay in the capture of John II. This foreclosed formal military activity but stimulated informal action by demobilized soldiers as France coped with crisis and civil war between the Dauphin and Charles de Navarre. Even the English may have kept up the pressure through unofficial activity: witness, for instance, the raids of Robert Knolles in the Auvergne. When negotiations dragged in the summer of 1359, Edward decided on a massive military action aimed at taking Reims, the royal crowning place.

Perhaps this was the only time in the war that Edward seriously considered taking the French throne, assisted by the captivity of John. This would certainly explain the army of 10,000, the largest since 1347 and possibly even the largest of the reign, with which he landed at Calais on 28 October 1359. Its composition was also interesting, in that it was almost wholly mounted, containing 4,000 men-at-arms and 5,000 archers, along with 700 foreign troops. Its ratio of men-at-arms to archers was almost 1:1, a departure from his campaigns of the 1340s but similar to those of the opening of the war. Almost the whole army was recruited by indentures with captains who brought along equal numbers of men-at-arms and archers. There was a great variation in the size of companies, from the 1,500 under the Black Prince to a company of nine under Sir Richard Pembridge.

This was the triumph of the professional 'mixed retinue', at the expense of infantry raised through the shire levies, who were needed at home in the face of diversionary raids commissioned by the Dauphin. English armies for the rest of the century followed this model.

Siege was laid to Reims on 4 December, and an assault attempted. But maintaining a long siege was difficult over the winter months. Such a large army needed too much food and was best kept on the move. But to where? Edward was unsure. There were several abortive moves

The capture of John II at the battle of Poitiers, where the English were commanded by the Black Prince, was a significant blow to the French. (Zip Lexing / Alamy Stock Photo)

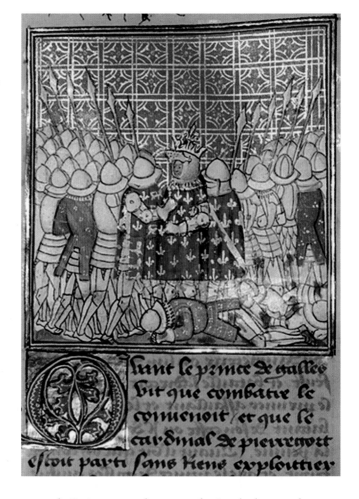

towards Paris even as late as early April: this was by now an exceptionally long time to have kept an army in the field. Edward decided to call it a day, being exceptionally short of victuals.

At Brétigny near Chartres on 8 May 1360, a treaty was struck giving Edward full sovereignty in Calais, Ponthieu, Poitou and an enlarged Aquitaine. In return he would refrain from calling himself King of France. Indeed, the ransom of three million écus that he had accepted for John confirmed the latter's right to rule. The kings met at Calais on 24 October to confirm the treaty.

The war was at an end. Edward had surely won this war, for he had gained what his predecessors could only have dreamed of – sovereign rule of half of France.

The second phase: 1369–99

Although England and France were technically at peace during the 1360s, soldiers from both countries were involved in various formal as well as *routier* activities. Civil war continued in Brittany until a force of English and Bretons under Sir John Chandos defeated and killed Charles de Blois at Auray on 29 September 1364. The French civil war with Charles de Navarre also dragged on until French constable Bertrand du Guesclin's victory at Cocherel on 16 May 1364.

But by far the most important theatre was Castile, where English and French intervened on behalf, respectively, of Pedro II and his half-brother, Henry of Trastamara. The most celebrated engagement was the Black Prince's victory at Nájera on 3 April 1367, not least because of the immense logistical achievement of taking an army through the Pyrenees. The prince's army consisted of three groups – 3,000 under Sir John Chandos and the prince's brother, John of Gaunt, Duke of Lancaster, deployed as the vanguard; the prince with his retinue; and members of the Great Company and of Pedro's troops in the main battle, numbering another 4,000 men. The lords of Armagnac and Albret held the right wing with 2,000 men and the Captal de Buch the left, with another 2,000. Trastamara's force was about 5,500, but was chaotically organized.

The prince took the Castilians by surprise by using a hill to mask his advance. He was able to prevent co-ordinated action between du Guesclin and Trastamara, and to impede the latter's advance by arrow fire. But the fierceness of the hand-to-hand fighting is revealed by the wound through Chandos's visor, which destroyed the sight in one eye.

The victory enhanced the prince's reputation but led to severe financial problems for him. The high tax that he

Sir John Chandos, portrayed here in William Bruges' Garter Book of 1435, was one of the founding knights of the Order in 1348 and was a prominent participant in the French wars. (Danvis Collection / Alamy Stock Photo)

subsequently placed on his principality of Aquitaine led to appeals to Charles V by Albret and Armagnac. This, as well as loopholes in the treaty of 1360, enabled Charles to claim the right to hear appeals as overlord and to the confiscation of English lands in November. Edward III initially tried to negotiate to avoid war, but on 3 June 1369 made war inevitable by resuming the title King of France.

It was announced that Charles, son of John, the former King of France, had usurped the sovereignty of the King of England … and had expelled him by his armies

(his banners having been unfurled) from his lands in
Ponthieu and elsewhere … and was still holding the same
in hostile fashion, and had assembled armed ships and
galleys in order to invade the kingdom of England and to
overthrow the king, thus making open war in a malicious
way against his oath and against the form of peace made
with the King of England. *(Roll of Parliament)*

In fact, hostilities had already broken out six months
earlier. The French took the English undefended
and by surprise, leading to early losses that made
Edward's resumed royal title an empty gesture. The
king's brother, Louis, Duke of Anjou, took Rouergue
and Quercy in early January 1369. Relations between
the Black Prince and his subjects had deteriorated so
far that Gascon assistance could no longer be relied
upon. Thus in January 1369 the English raised a small
expeditionary force under Edward's fourth son, the Earl
of Cambridge, and the Earl of Pembroke, which came
to the rescue of English possessions in Périgord.

In April, the French entered Abbeville, capital of
Ponthieu. The English had despatched 250 troops
there in February, but they were too few to hold the
area. The fall of Ponthieu raised concerns over Calais, so
that other troops intended for Gascony were diverted to
Calais in May, and a new captain, Gaunt's son, the Earl
of Hereford, appointed with 900 men.

Edward III realized that a major demonstration of
military might was needed. He thus planned to campaign
himself in northern France, and began to negotiate with
allies for troops. About 1,000 men from Brabant and
Juliers joined with Gaunt, who was sent ahead of his
father to Calais in late July 1369 with 2,000 to counter
French attacks on England. The English, not threatened
for many decades, had let their home defences slip. Thus
from mid-June there was a flurry of orders to fortify
Thanet, Portsmouth (which was attacked in September),
Southampton and Portchester, with the shire levies also
being called out in July. The English launched a short raid
on Sainte-Addresse, the ports of Upper Normandy being

Bertrand du Guesclin was constable of France from 1370 and instrumental in reviving French fortunes. He had the honour of burial in the royal necropolis of Saint-Denis close to the tomb of Charles V. (Photo by Photo12/ UIG/Getty Images)

the likely place from which any attack on England would be made. There were even fears that the French might enter through Wales with the aid of the inhabitants: on 24 December, Edward instructed lords with lands there to see to their safekeeping.

The intention was that Gaunt should harry Picardy and Thérouanne in standard *chevauchée* style. He came close to battle with Charles's brother, Philip, Duke of Burgundy, at Tournehem on 23 August, but only a skirmish occurred. Gaunt then fell back to Calais in September. By the middle of the month another 2,000-strong army under the Earls of Warwick, March, Salisbury and Oxford landed at Calais. Edward was not with them, probably because of the death of his wife on 15 August, although he may have decided to stay in England in case the French did invade.

The actions of this composite army under Gaunt's overall command show that the English aimed to attack the areas from which invasion might come. It carried out a campaign of devastation in Upper Normandy, being assisted by the English fleet, which harried the coast. In October the army returned to Calais before the end of its contract. Gaunt had been cautious and limited in his actions, but the threat of invasion had indeed been averted.

In the following year, a more audacious move was planned. Four thousand men were contracted under Sir Robert Knolles for two years' service. The plan was to allow Knolles to emulate the activities of the *routiers*, taking pay only for the first three months and then letting his force live off the land, conducting raids when and wherever necessary. Knolles' first action was a fast and damaging *chevauchée* from Calais around the east of Paris and thence to Poitou and Brittany. But his rearguard was ambushed by du Guesclin near Le Mans, and the army disbanded only six months into its contract. Du Guesclin had already demonstrated his skill in weakening the effectiveness of the *chevauchée* by deploying his troops in flanking actions to delimit the path of the English, and to prevent any conquests.

OPPOSITE

Charles V's position was boosted by a visit from the Emperor Charles IV in 1374. Here the two rulers are portrayed at a banquet in Paris. The martial scene on the right may be a reminder of their hopes for a joint crusade against the Saracens. (Bibliothèque Nationale de France)

His leadership and influence were to be key to French successes of the next decade. He played a fundamental role in Charles V's battle-avoiding strategy which deprived the English of any chance of a victory in the field. Although being from humble social origins, his importance was recognized by his burial close to the king in Saint-Denis in 1380.

The French under the Duke of Anjou continued their advances in the south-west in 1370, taking the Agenais, Limousin and Buzac. Furious that the bishop of Limoges had entered into negotiations with the French, the Black Prince rushed to sack the city, an act most certainly against the conventions of war and chivalry. By now he was seriously ill, and returned to England in 1371, dying in 1376. The defence of English Aquitaine, or what was left of it, was entrusted to Gaunt, but only small forces of 500 and 800 men were sent for his support.

French penetration of Saintonge and Poitou prompted the dispatch of the Earl of Pembroke in April 1372 with 1,500 men and enough money to raise an army of 3,000 in Gascony. But his transport fleet had only three armed escorts to guard it, and was intercepted by Castilian galleys off La Rochelle. On 23 June, the Castilians sent flaming arrows into English ships caught in the shallows of the harbour. Virtually the whole fleet was lost. La Rochelle fell on 8 September. Equally galling was the fact that the money for the Gascon troops was at the bottom of the sea. The defeat also thwarted plans for Edward III to cross from Southampton with a force of 4,000 (the intended location of this campaign is not clear). Instead, the troops were sent to sea against the threat of further French naval action, although none materialized.

Thus in 1372 the English position already looked very bleak. There was only one glimmer of hope – a renewed alliance with the Duke of Brittany in June 1372, although this led to the confiscation of his duchy and its occupation by French troops. An advance army of 600 men under John, Lord Neville, landed there in October. It was in the following year that the English raised their largest army of this second phase, 6,000 strong, and

premierement fist laurenels
de Reins Apres seoit
lempereur Apres seoit
le Roy ausreibme en miheu
du front de la sale Apres
le Roy de france seoir le roy

des romains. Et auoit auteur de distance
du Roy au Roy des romains come du
Roy a lempereur. Et auoient lempereur
le Roy et le Roy des romains chascun se
parement un ciel de drap dor bade de urla
au aus armes de france. et par dessus ceul

THE TREATY OF BRÉTIGNY/CALAIS
(1360) AND THE CAMPAIGNS OF
THE SECOND PHASE OF THE WAR

Bruges

CALAIS
Roosebeke
(1382)
Tournehem
Ypres

PONTHIEU

Cherbourg

Cocherel
(1364)

Brest

Rennes

Auray
(1364)   Vannes

Nantes

POITOU

La Rochelle
(1372)

SAINTONGE

LIMOUSIN

AQUITAINE

Bordeaux

N

GASCONY

Toulouse

BEARN

Chevauchée of John of Gaunt, Duke of Lancaster, 1369
Chevauchée of Sir Robert Knolles, 1370
Chevauchée of John of Gaunt, Duke of Lancaster, 1373
Chevauchée of Thomas Woodstock, 1380
'Crusade' under Bishop Despencer of Norwich, 1383
Lands held by Edward III in full sovereignty as a result
of the treaty of Brétigny/Calais, 1360

0   100 miles

0   100 km

containing the dukes of Lancaster and Brittany as well as three earls, 12 foreign captains and nearly 250 knights. The intention was to effect a great *chevauchée* from Calais to Artois and Champagne. Not surprisingly, this caused consternation to the French, but Gaunt then decided to turn south to reinforce the position in Gascony rather than moving on Paris.

Why was no move made by either side towards a battle? Throughout this phase of the war, Charles V was not prepared to run the risk, even if this meant that English armies could raid without much constraint. There is little indication that the English were keen on engagement. The expeditionary forces they despatched between 1369 and 1380 were all of mounted men alone, and with men-at-arms and archers in the ratio of 1:1. Thus they were more suited to raiding than to battle formation, where the lack of archers would have made them vulnerable. This contributed to the stalemate of the phase.

Stalemate also arose in the territorial position once La Réole surrendered to the French in 1374, reducing the English to the Gascony of 1337. The sending of regular small companies from England during the later 1370s to hold the garrisons and launch occasional sorties on the frontier made it difficult for the French to penetrate further. In 1375, the English decided to concentrate their efforts on Brittany, raising an army of 4,000 under the Earl of Cambridge and the Duke of Brittany. Its actions were cut short by a papally initiated truce, but when war reopened in 1377, du Guesclin and the Duke of Anjou began to penetrate Gascony, besieging Bergerac. The town fell on 2 September, and other towns along the Dordogne soon followed. Several Gascon lords defected, but Bordeaux was saved by counter-actions under John Neville.

Even so, the English position in 1377 was perhaps weaker than ever. The French launched serious raids on the south coast, facilitated by the recent establishment of a royal shipbuilding yard at Rouen. The English position was not assisted by the death of Edward III on 21 June 1377, and the accession of his ten-year-old grandson, Richard II.

Further disasters followed. A 4,000-strong force for Brittany in 1379 was reduced to 1,300 and then destroyed by sea storms off Cornwall and Ireland. In 1380, Edward III's youngest son, Thomas of Woodstock, Earl of Buckingham, led 4,000 along the, by now, customary *chevauchée* route from Calais through Champagne, Beauce and Anjou to Brittany, before laying siege to Nantes for two months without success. The Duke of Brittany came to an agreement with the French on 15 January 1381, and remained largely neutral in the war thenceforward.

After 1380, the English sent no large expeditionary forces to France: the expense that they generated had not been matched by their achievements. But a presence was maintained in Brittany, for Brest had been leased from the Duke of Brittany 'for the duration of the war with France', and Cherbourg from the King of Navarre. These usually housed 100 men, along with a good quantity of ordnance.

It was during this second phase of the war that the value of gunpowder artillery was first seen, at the French recovery of Saint-Sauveur-le Vicomte in 1375. Brest housed at least nine guns, with more brought over from England when the French laid siege in 1386. Cherbourg had ten guns, seven firing 24-in. (61cm) stones, and three 15-in. (38cm) stones. But these were but pinpricks in what was otherwise an ever-strengthening French position, and the English failed in their attempts to take other bridgeheads in France such as Saint-Malo, Harfleur and La Rochelle. This was partly because the French had done much from the 1360s onwards to ensure the maintenance of fortifications.

After 1380, the English concentrated their military endeavours outside France. The hope of exploiting the Flemish alliance was dealt a blow by the French defeat of the townsmen at Roosebeke on 27 November 1382. The English were only able to finance an army in the following year by launching it as a crusade against those who supported a schismatic pope. This way taxation could be levied from the church to pay for it. Bishop

Despencer of Norwich's force managed to take the coast between Gravelines and Blankenberghe and to lay siege to Ypres, but the advance of the Duke of Burgundy prompted his withdrawal.

There was failure for Gaunt in Castile in 1386, and the expedition that Richard II had led to Scotland in 1385, made financially viable only by resurrecting the royal right to free service in the feudal levy, was not enough to keep the Scots at bay. In 1388, they invaded again, winning a victory in battle at Otterburn on 5 August. In 1386–87, the French laid siege to Brest. This prompted what was in effect a naval *chevauchée* under Arundel in 1387, with a further sea-borne campaign in 1388.

These were the last campaigns of this phase of the war. A short truce agreed on 18 June 1389 led in time to a 28-year truce in March 1396, cemented by

The castle of Saint-Sauveur-le-Vicomte in the Cotentin was held by Sir John Chandos in the mid-14th century and fell into English hands again in the conquests of Henry V. (Ikmoned, Wikimedia Commons, CC BY-SA 3.0)

the marriage of Richard II to Charles VI's daughter on 4 November. Cherbourg was handed back in 1393, and Brest in 1397. The English now held only the Gascony of 1337 and Calais.

The English military effort required in this phase was exceptionally intensive and expensive, with over 30,000 troops raised for expeditionary armies between 1369 and 1380. Evidence suggests that the armies were well organized and disciplined, yet they achieved little because of the nature of the campaigns and the numbers of theatres in which the English had to engage. The French were better prepared for attack, and had won much advantage by their swift actions in 1369. In addition to reforming company sizes and discipline, Charles V had initiated a system of provision of troops by parishes in the early 1360s against the *routiers*. This gave the French 3,000 troops on standby.

Why, then, were the French not able to effect a total victory? The answer lies in the strains that they also began to feel around 1380, with tax rebellions and increasing political divisions during the minority of Charles VI. A stalemate thus arose, in which a long truce was acceptable to both sides. This might have signalled the end of the war had it not been for the outbreak of civil war between the Burgundians and Orléanists (or Armagnacs) in the wake of Charles's growing insanity, and the change of circumstances in England following the deposition of Richard II in 1399.

The third phase: 1399–1429

Although technically the truce was maintained until Henry V invaded in August 1415, the circumstances of the first 15 years of the 15th century are best portrayed as cold war. There was disquiet amongst some Gascons at the usurpation of Henry IV, but this was subdued by a small, but prompt military showing by the English. From 1403 the French launched several incursions under Louis, Duke of Orléans. Losses were incurred in the Agenais, towards Saintonge and on the

OPPOSITE
Richard II, the first English king for whom a contemporary portrait survives, came to a long truce with the French, marrying Isabella, the young daughter of Charles VI, in 1396. (Photo by Fine Art Images/ Heritage Images/ Getty Images)

OPPOSITE
This portrait of
Henry V is derived
from a painting
of the early 16th
century produced
for Henry VII or
Henry VIII, and
was much copied.
(Photo by: Universal
History Archive/
Universal Images
Group via Getty
Images)

frontier with Périgord. Bordeaux itself was threatened when sieges were laid to Bourg and Blaye, but these proved abortive in the early months of 1407. In November of that same year the danger receded when the Duke of Orléans was assassinated at the order of John, Duke of Burgundy.

The ensuing escalation of the French civil war made Henry IV aware that French weakness could work to his benefit. Negotiations recommenced, but, more importantly, both the Burgundians and the Armagnacs sought English aid in their own struggle. In October 1411, a force of 800 men-at-arms and 2,000 archers under the Earl of Arundel was sent to assist Burgundy at the behest of Henry, Prince of Wales.

In the summer of 1412, a full-scale army of 1,000 men-at-arms and 3,000 archers was despatched at the king's order to aid the Armagnacs, who had promised in return to honour the terms of Brétigny. This army was commanded by the king's second son, Thomas, Duke of Clarence, accompanied by his cousin Edward, Duke of York, and his uncle Thomas Beaufort, Earl of Dorset (later Duke of Exeter). All three later served in the Agincourt campaign. The army landed at Saint-Vaast-la-Hougue, as Edward III had done in 1346, and carried out some raids into Normandy. It then moved towards de Blois where it was to join with the Armagnacs, but was bought off when the two sides in the civil war came to an agreement. Clarence then led his men to Bordeaux before returning to England.

There can be little doubt that Henry V was encouraged in his own aggressive stance towards France by these precedents and by the opportunities offered by French internal divisions. His hard line in diplomacy was matched by his major military effort to launch an expedition in 1415. The army raised numbered over 12,000, and was notable for the extremely large number of men, over 500, who indented to bring troops. This was truly the nation at war. Most of the active peerage served. The king's two brothers, the dukes of Clarence and Gloucester, led companies of 960 and 800 men

respectively, with the royal household also forming a large division: even men such as the surveyor of the works at the royal palaces, or the porter of the hall, brought along small retinues. Even more notable were the many esquires and yeomen who indented in person with a handful of archers.

The ratio of all the retinues was also distinctive, at one man-at-arms to three archers, a notable increase in the proportion of archers compared with the campaigns of the two 14th-century phases of the war. In addition, there were companies of 500 archers from Lancashire, Wales and Cheshire, all with close links to the crown. This ratio is first seen in the campaigns in Wales. It would be tempting to say that it was testimony to the realisation of the firepower of archers, but it was more likely moved by the fact that archers cost half the daily wage of a man-at-arms – a significant factor when Henry had cash to pay for only the first three of 12 months' intended service, and had to provide jewels as security for the following three months.

Whereas Henry IV had concentrated his efforts on Gascony, his son launched a new enterprise aimed at Normandy. It is highly likely that the first expedition of 1415 was aimed at conquest. But the siege of Harfleur took longer than anticipated and Henry lost some of his army to disease. He also needed to place 1,200 men into garrison once Harfleur fell, since it had been so damaged by his bombardement. Nonetheless, he still had over 8,000 men under his command. He marched them northwards to Calais, intending to cross the Somme where Edward III had crossed in 1346. This march was not a *chevauchée* of the 14th-century type since Henry was careful to restrain his troops, although towns such as Eu could hardly refuse to supply victuals in order to escape damage.

On reaching the Somme, fearing the presence of a large French army on the north bank Henry was forced to march around 80 km inland to find a safe crossing of the river. Once he had managed to cross, the French summoned him to battle, with the planned engagement

THE AGINCOURT CAMPAIGN, 1415

Calais
(28 Oct)

Canche

Agincourt
(25 Oct)

Maisoncelle
Hesdin

St Pol

Aubigny-en-Artois

Arras

Cambrai

Frevent

Crécy

Authie

Blanchetaque
(13 Oct)

Abbeville
(14 Oct)

Doullens
(23 Oct)

Bapaume
20 Oct

Eu
(12 Oct)

Somme

Acheux

Albert

Peronne
(21 Oct)

Dieppe

11 Oct

St Quentin

10 Oct

Bresle

(15 Oct)

Amiens
17 Oct

Corbie

Athies
(20 Oct)

Arques
(11 Oct)

Béthune

Boves
(16 Oct)

Caix

Voyennes
(19 Oct)

Fécamp
(9 Oct)

9 Oct

Nesle
(18 Oct)

Somme

(13 Aug)

Caudebec
(8 Oct)

Harfleur
(8 Oct)

Gournay

Honfleur

Rouen
14 Oct

Beauvais

Compiègne

Aisne

Seine

Gisors

Senlis

Soissons

Lisieux

Bernay

Vernon

Evreux

Bonnières

Mantes

Paris

Meaux

Marne

Dreux

Oise

N

0		50 miles
0		100 km

→ Route of the English army
→ Route of the French main army
⇢ Route of the French advance guard
13 Aug French army
(13 Aug) English army

This image of the battle of Agincourt, from a version of Monstrelet's *Chroniques* of the mid-15th century, presents a rather inaccurate portrayal, since the composition of the armies was quite different, with the French failing to deploy their crossbowmen and such few longbowmen as they had. (GRANGER - Historical Picture Archive / Alamy Stock Photo)

probably intended to be at Aubigny in Artois. The route Henry then chose suggests he was trying still to avoid battle, but when he reached Agincourt, around 40km south of Calais, he found a French army waiting for him. Henry's order, made close to Corbie as he marched along the Somme, that his archers should prepare stakes

was made in anticipation not of battle, but of ambush by the French, who were stalking him all the way as well as preparing a major army at Rouen in the hope of revenging themselves for Poitiers: their army was equally lustrous in terms of the participation of the peerage, and numbered around 12,000. But this was not to be.

Although it was the French who chose to bring Henry to battle at Agincourt on 25 October, he was able to exploit the natural features of the site to funnel and control their attack. Key to his success were the 7,000 or so archers in his company. But it also seems that not all the planned French army had managed to arrive in time.

The French plan, which still survives and which was probably devised for an intended battle closer to the mouth of the Somme, included an intended cavalry charge against the archers, which might indeed have taken them out. But the charge was limited, and the English archers were thus able to harry the main French foot advance. Accounts of the battle suggest that the French lost their momentum, became too closely packed to use their weapons, and piled on top of each other, where they were easy pickings for men-at-arms and archers alike. Only on the English right, commanded by the Duke of York, were they able to wreak much damage on the English. The carnage on the French side was significant, with important prisoners being captured, not least Charles VI's nephew, Charles, Duke of Orléans, leader of the Armagnac faction, who was not released from his English captivity until 1440. Yet we must be mindful of the fact that Henry had been uncertain enough of victory to order the killing of prisoners when he feared a renewed French attack. The battle of Agincourt was by no means decisive. Neither the French king nor the Dauphin had been present, nor had John the Fearless, Duke of Burgundy. But the latter was able to exploit the demise of his political enemy, the Duke of Orléans, and within the next few years gained control of both Paris and the increasingly mentally incapacitated king.

In the opinion of the French, it was what injured them the most which assured the English of victory, especially the continuous hail of arrow shot which rained down on our men. As the English archers were lightly armed and their ranks not too crowded, they had freedom of movement and could deal mortal blows with ease. Many of them had adopted a weapon until then unknown – great lead-covered mallets from which one blow to the head could kill a man or knock him senseless to the ground. *(Chronicle of the Religieux of Saint-Denis)*

Less remembered but equally significant for Henry's plans was the naval victory of his brother, John, Duke of Bedford, over the French and their Genoese allies in the mouth of the Seine on 15 August 1416. This battle was hard fought, lasting around seven hours. But for the English it secured the safety of Harfleur, and facilitated Henry's second campaign by weakening French maritime defences. On 1 August 1417 he landed again in Normandy, at the mouth of the Touques. This time his intended systematic conquest met with complete success. Caen withstood siege for two weeks. Henry then moved south to take Alençon and other places on the frontier with Maine.

Once Falaise fell in February 1418, after a siege of over two months, Lower Normandy was divided into two by the English conquest, and Henry could divide his forces for campaigns to the west and east. The Cotentin fell swiftly save for Cherbourg, which held out for five months until September 1418. The area towards the Seine fell by mid-summer, and Henry began his siege of Rouen in late July. Rouen held out for six months, but once it was in English hands, the remainder of Upper Normandy fell with little resistance. By the summer of 1419 virtually the whole of the duchy was in Henry's hands, with English garrisons distributed in key points.

Henry had been assisted by an army in 1417 of around 12,000, with reinforcements crossing in subsequent years. With such numbers, and with experienced commanders of high status, he had been able to employ a multi-pronged approach, thereby speeding up the conquest. His use of artillery is also notable, as defences were inadequate to resist bombardment. Henry consciously distributed lands to his soldiers, demanding in return both defensive and offensive military obligations, thus giving many a vested interest in maintaining and extending the conquest. This

It was in the Cathedral of St Pierre in Troyes, still under construction, that an Anglo-French treaty was agreed on 21 May 1420, between Henry V and Queen Isabeau, acting as representative of her husband Charles VI. (Christine944/Getty Images)

was a new and imaginative ploy, reinforced by his good treatment of the Normans. He also established a garrison system in Normandy, ensuring sound defence of key towns and castles, and also ensuring enough troops to patrol the countryside around.

There seems little doubt that Henry's war aim was to take and hold Normandy. That was the focus of his negotiations with the French in 1419, but his ambitions were boosted when the civil war took another turn for the worse. Duke John of Burgundy had taken advantage of the English attack to take Paris in May 1418, and control of the mad king. Efforts to reconcile him with the Armagnacs, now led by the Dauphin Charles, came to nothing when he was assassinated at Montereau on 10 September 1419. This led directly to an Anglo-

Burgundian alliance and to Henry increasing his war aims to the crown itself. By the Treaty of Troyes of May 1420 he became heir and regent of Charles VI.

One of the clauses of the treaty committed Henry to making war on the Dauphin and the Armagnacs until all of France accepted the treaty. This was a tall order as Henry's last two years revealed.

Even close to Paris, there were places that resisted: Henry spent most of his last years in France in sieges to the east of the capital. The siege of Meaux, his last engagement where he contracted dysentery, began in October 1421 and lasted until March 1422. The move southwards by the Duke of Clarence had led to his death in battle at Baugé on 22 March 1421, a battle that saw further important casualties and prisoners.

Henry's early demise in 1422 did not make the matter any easier. Many places supported the Dauphin. Mont-Saint-Michel, for instance, was never captured despite several sieges by land and sea, and even within Normandy and the Ile de France, the Armagnacs recovered places from time to time. The Dauphin was assisted by Scottish troops, although two major blows were served to his cause by the defeats suffered at Cravant (31 July 1423) and Verneuil (17 August 1424). The latter opened the way for an offensive into Maine, which fell to the English over 1425–28, and then to the Loire, culminating in the siege of Orléans laid in October 1428.

Throughout the 1420s the English had sent regular expeditionary forces to France, and had also been able to draw on valuable military assistance from the Burgundians, who had themselves developed an impressive military and artillery presence. What is particularly notable about this period of the war is the strong defensive provision in the form of garrisons placed throughout Normandy and the other areas under Anglo-Burgundian authority. These followed the precedents laid down by Henry V, and were well organized during the regency of John, Duke of Bedford, being administered through French systems and financed through local taxation. Considerable attention

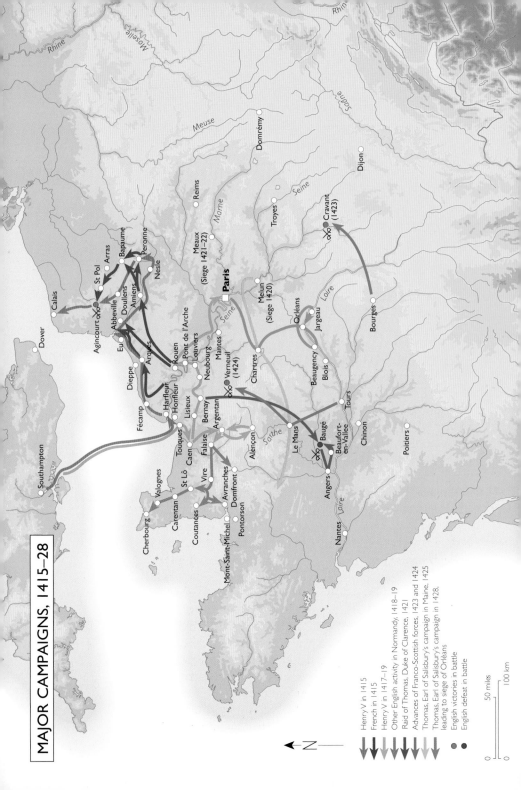

MAJOR CAMPAIGNS, 1415–28

Rhine

Moselle

Rhine

Meuse

Sambre

Domrémy

Dijon

Reims

Troyes

Seine

Cravant (1423)

Bourges

Calais

Dover

St Pol

Arras

Bapaume

Péronne

Nesle

Amiens

Doullens

Abbeville

Agincourt

Eu

Arques

Dieppe

Rouen

Pont de l'Arche

Louviers

Neubourg

Mantes

Meaux (Siege 1421–22)

Paris

Melun (Siege 1420)

Orléans

Jargeau

Loire

Beaugency

Blois

Southampton

Fécamp

Harfleur

Honfleur

Lisieux

Touques

Caen

St Lô

Vire

Falaise

Bernay

Argentan

Alençon

Verneuil (1424)

Chartres

Le Mans

Baugé

Beaufort-en-Vallée

Tours

Chinon

Poitiers

Cherbourg

Valognes

Carentan

Coutances

Avranches

Domfront

Mont-Saint-Michel

Pontorson

Sarthe

Angers

Nantes

Loire

N

0   50 miles

0   100 km

Henry V in 1415

French in 1415

Henry V in 1417–19

Other English activity in Normandy, 1418–19

Raid of Thomas, Duke of Clarence, 1421

Advances of Franco-Scottish forces, 1423 and 1424

Thomas, Earl of Salisbury's campaign in Maine, 1425

Thomas, Earl of Salisbury's campaign in 1428, leading to siege of Orléans

English victories in battle

English defeat in battle

was paid to the maintenance of military discipline and to good relations with the civilian population, as it had been under Henry V. The English made much effort to win hearts and minds, especially in Normandy, by rewarding and protecting those civilians who were willing to enter into English allegiance. In particular, they developed strong disciplinary codes for their soldiers which controlled the taking of victuals, and also ordered a series of inquiries into abuses. As a result both were praised, and they were able from January 1421 to call the Estates of Normandy almost every year to raise taxation within the duchy to support the cost of garrisons. This took the pressure off English taxation. No tax grant was asked for in England between 1422 and 1429.

The fourth phase: 1429–53

The victory at Verneuil had enabled the English to scale down their garrisons in Normandy from over 4,000 to just over 2,000 men, as well as to send armies to secure Maine, the province which lay to the south of Normandy. Garrisons were installed and lands distributed as in Normandy, along with efforts to persuade the local population to accept the double monarchy. The greatest extent of loyalty to the double monarchy, with Burgundian assistance, was secured by the autumn of 1428. It was then decided to carry out a push southwards into the Dauphin's territories south of the Loire. Siege was laid to Orléans in October 1429 with around 4,000 troops but the English suffered an early blow in the death of Thomas, Earl of Salisbury, from a gunshot fired from one of the towers of the bridge. The siege continued into the spring, the English managing to bring in much needed victuals thanks to success at the 'battle of the Herrings' at Rouvray on 12 February 1429. But in April the Burgundians withdrew their supporting troops. In the following month Joan of Arc, with a French forward force under the Count of Dunois, was able to enter Orléans from the east, indicating that the English

This intriguing doodle of Joan of Arc was made in the margin of the Register of the Parlement of Paris against an entry recording her first action at the siege of Orleans, to which a gloss was later added concerning her capture at Compiègne a year later. (The Picture Art Collection / Alamy Stock Photo)

blockade had not been effective. With urban support and French reinforcements, the siege was lifted and the English moved away from the town.

The French, whose numbers are unclear, now carried all before them, defeating the English in pitched battle at Patay on 18 June 1429, where the English archers were encircled by the French cavalry charge. Two leading English commanders, the Earl of Suffolk and John, Lord Talbot, were captured. The French then conducted a veritable *blitzkrieg*, capturing many places en route to Reims, where the Dauphin was crowned on 17 July as Charles VII.

Paris was itself under threat. It is fair to say that the Anglo-Burgundians had felt so secure in their conquests that they had made little defensive provision once they had started the advance towards the Loire. The evidence we have of English military activity in 1429–30 shows just how much energy and money had to be expended on the defence of Paris and the Norman frontiers. The garrison establishment was increased from 2,000 men to 3,500, and extra companies were installed in the vulnerable places on the eastern frontier.

Paris was saved, largely because Charles lost his nerve and the English poured in over 7,000 troops from England during 1430–31. The English were thus able to prevent further losses. Louviers was recovered after two long sieges, thus returning most of Normandy to English hands. Joan was captured and removed from the scene in May 1431 after her trial at Rouen. The young king Henry VI was then able to travel in some safety to Paris for his coronation in December 1431.

But whilst the early 1430s saw some consolidation, the strains of the years 1429–31 continued to tell, not least in war finances and in the need to maintain defence. It soon became apparent that the English could not hope to extend their territory. Even in Normandy, French incursions began to increase. This most certainly heightened anti-English feeling in the duchy and contributed to the revolt of the peasants of the pays de Caux in 1435 and the French penetration of much of Upper Normandy, including the key ports of Dieppe and Harfleur. This forced the English on to the defensive once more, and restricted their war aims to the recovery of the lost areas of the duchy. Shortly before the revolt, the Duke of Burgundy finally declared his true colours and came to a treaty with Charles VII at Arras. A week earlier, the Duke of Bedford had died at Rouen. The year 1435 was surely the English *annus horribilis*, and 1436 promised to be no better when Burgundy laid siege to Calais, and Paris fell to Charles.

GARRISON DETACHMENTS SERVING IN THE FIELD, 1424

- English garrisons sending detachments for *journée* (battle) of Verneuil, August 1424
- **St-Lô** English garrisons sending detachments for siege of Mont-Saint-Michel, Sept 1424–June 1425
- ⚓ Places sending ships for siege of Mont-Saint-Michel by sea, April–June 1425

London

Guernsey

Cherbourg

Valognes

Pont-d'Ouve

Carentan

Neuilly-l'Evêque

Bayeux

Gavray

St-Lô

Coutances

Regneville

Granville

Genêts

Tombelaine

Mont-Saint-Michel ⚓

Pontorson

Ardenvon

Avranches

St-James-de-Beuvron

Domfront

Vire

Caen ⚓

Falaise

Argentan

Exmes

Lisieux

Orbec

Bernay

Essay

Alençon

Bellême

Fresnay

Longny

Verneuil ⚔

Conches

Evreux

Dreux

Mantes

Meulan

Poissy

St Germain

Pontoise

La Roche-Guyon

Gisors

Chateau-Gaillard

Vernon

Pont-de-l'Arche

Louviers

Elbeuf

Gournay

Rouen

Pont-Audemer

Pont l'Evêque

Honfleur

Touques

Harfleur

Montivilliers

Tancarville

Caudebec

Montivilliers

Neufchâtel

Gerberoy

Eu

Dieppe

Arques

Torcy

N

0 ___ 25 miles

0 ___ 50 km

Again it is perhaps surprising that the English held on and that the war did not end at this point. That it did not is testimony to the massive military effort that the English made in 1436, sending a total of around 10,000 troops to the defence of Calais and to Normandy, where the garrison establishment was raised to its highest level of almost 7,500. The English were also helped by Burgundian disinterest and by Charles's caution. This enabled them to recover much of what they had lost in Normandy. Harfleur, an important symbol of English conquest, was recovered in November 1440.

But a defensive position is never easy to maintain. The French held on to Dieppe, placing a garrison of over 1,000 men there at the time of the English siege of 1442. They also held Evreux and Louviers from 1440, forcing a wedge into the English position south of the Seine. Moreover, war damage and economic crisis in Normandy combined to make the pays de Caux a depopulated and unprofitable area. Taxation income fell, whilst defence costs increased. Large numbers of troops from England continued to be needed. Between 1440 and 1443, over 13,000 were sent.

Gascony had been largely devoid of conflict until the late 1430s as both English and French concentrated on the northern lands. The English government's interest in Gascony was renewed in 1439 when there was the possibility of a peace settlement. England now wished to ensure that Gascony's boundaries were as extensive as possible. Thus an expeditionary force of over 2,000 – the largest since 1412 – was sent under the Earl of Huntingdon. Charles VII responded by fortifying the fortresses of the Lord of Albret. Initially, Huntingdon's advance met with success, but he was recalled in 1440. In 1442, Charles launched an invasion, taking Dax and St Sever.

The English responded slowly. Interests in Normandy and in Gascony began to compete for resources. Initially, it was planned that John Beaufort, Earl of Somerset, should cross to Gascony with a force

Dece qui leur advint depuis.

Ilz tenoient en ladicte Ville.

An important turning point in the reign of Charles VII was the booting out of the English from Paris in April 1436, as portrayed in a celebration of the king's life produced by Martial d'Auvergne in 1484. (Photo by Art Media/Print Collector/Getty Images)

of 800 men-at-arms and 3,400 archers (the increased proportion of archers being a clear indication of the financial difficulties in which the English crown found itself), but his charge was subsequently changed to Normandy, and he crossed in 1443 with 800 troops fewer than his indenture had demanded. His strategy of taking the war to the French on the frontiers of Brittany was a complete failure, and had deprived not only Gascony but also Dieppe, to which siege was then being laid, of much needed succour.

This was the last expedition to France. On 28 May 1444, the English agreed a truce with the French, the first cessation of hostilities since 1415. Between these

dates, therefore, we have the longest continuous period of conflict of the whole of the Hundred Years War.

The English felt so secure at Dieppe that by 1435, only four men-at-arms and 12 archers were stationed there. The castle fell easily to the French in December that year. (Patrick, Flickr, CC BY-SA 2.0)

THE WORLD AROUND WAR
War cruel and sharp

A war against civilians?

A very important point can be made about the nature of warfare in the Hundred Years War. Most of it, whether on land or at sea, was conducted within a civilian context. Only battles were restricted to the professional soldiery. The *chevauchée* was chosen because it was against soft, civilian targets and could have an immediate, demoralising effect. Soldiers on the move ate their way through an area, and took moveable booty as well as burning stored crops and houses. Fortified centres and engagements with enemy troops were generally avoided. It was extremely difficult to respond effectively enough, in that the attackers swiftly moved on to their next target, and communication problems made military intelligence less effective. No one quite knew with *chevauchées* where the attacker would move next. Sieges both involved and affected civilians. Lengthy sieges were particularly harsh on the inhabitants of large towns. We are told that the citizens had to eat dogs, cats and even vermin during the six-month siege of Rouen over the winter of 1418–19.

War was deliberately taken to the people. Such actions against civilians might be deemed legitimate acts of war as they had been licensed by the king. But there were many other acts of destruction and disruption carried

OPPOSITE

The splendid west front of Rouen Cathedral. The city experienced a harsh siege laid by Henry V from July 1418 to January 1419. (Patrick, Flickr, CC BY-SA 2.0)

out by soldiers of their own volition. Garrison soldiers of both sides often went out 'on their own adventure', and no doubt were given some freedom in deciding from whom booty could be taken, despite disciplinary ordinances for both armies which tried to prevent their attacking civilians. Piracy was encouraged by both the English and French, not least during the period of truce in the late 14th and early 15th centuries.

In France there was also the problem of the lawless bands known in the 14th century as the *routiers*, who continued the war against civilians when they found themselves out of regular military employment. To this we must add the impact of two extremely bitter and violent civil wars, namely between the Dauphin and Charles de Navarre in the late 1350s, which had a particularly marked effect in the Paris Basin, and between the Armagnacs and Burgundians in the early 15th century. Both became enmeshed with the Anglo-French war. At base, it was French war failures that encouraged public disorder and infighting. But in the 15th century we also find French freedom fighters operating as *écorcheurs* and *brigans* in order to undermine English rule of France.

Effects on France

It was hard to believe that this was the country I had seen in the past … I could hardly recognize anything that I had seen before in this kingdom which was once so rich and which was now reduced to ashes. *(Petrarch, commenting on the state of France)*

There can be little doubt that France was severely damaged physically and economically by the Hundred Years War. The very title of Henri Deniflé's influential book published between 1897 and 1899, *La désolation des églises, monastères et hopitaux en France pendant la Guerre de cent ans*, epitomizes the approach taken and the conclusions drawn, with not even the church being exempt from attack, especially by the *routiers*. Detailed studies of the Ile-de-France, the Auvergne and Anjou, as well as of major cities such as Toulouse, Tours, Poitiers and Périgueux, have confirmed this view. The values of rents in rural Anjou, for instance, fell by 30–40 per cent over the second half of the 14th century.

A study of Reims is particularly indicative, not least because the city saw a siege by Edward III in 1359 as well as the disturbances of the Navarrese civil war and later English *chevauchées*. Over many decades, peasants flocked into the city for protection, swelling some parishes by 50 per cent. Prices of cereals rocketed: the situation was particularly bad in the late 1350s and 1360s when military actions disrupted the usual trade with towns in the vicinity. The fortification of Reims in the 1350s cost over 100,000 *livres tournois*, much of it sustained out of local purchase taxes, and involved the demolition of dwellings and religious establishments in the suburbs and in the surrounding area to create a *cordon sanitaire*.

Although there was some recovery in the early 15th century, conditions worsened in the fourth phase of the war. French incursions into Gascony from the early 1440s destroyed vines, which took years of regrowth to recover. In Normandy, the battle for the pays de Caux after 1435 led to economic crisis, not least for the ports. The hinterlands of Harfleur and Dieppe were devastated by English armies sent in to recover these places. At Dieppe, the suburb of *Le pollet outre l'eau* (on the other side of the harbour from the main town) was virtually deserted in 1437–38, its residents having 'gone to live elsewhere because of the war'. The English subsequently placed their siege camp there in 1442–43, after which the area was noted as 'completely demolished and ruinous'. It proved impossible to attract the inhabitants back until the English had been driven out of the duchy.

A study of Louviers reveals the damaging effects of recurrent sieges: the town changed hands five times between 1418 and 1440. Revenues from tolls on grain fell from £29 in 1424 to £13 in 1432, with the total

value of the town falling from over £191 to £115 over the same period. After the French took the town in 1440 they demolished the cloth hall so that its materials could be used in rebuilding the outer fortifications. Declining rents and agricultural production in the late 1430s and 1440s were so marked that Guy Bois went so far as to term it 'Hiroshima in Normandy', although he admitted that not all economic problems were due to the war. Such circumstances affected not only Normans but also the occupier, for many English had been granted lands in the duchy which were now often of little or no value. Sir John Fastolf, for instance, lost a third of his income of £600 from his French lands as a result of the loss of the pays de Caux and the subsequent economic crisis.

Little now survives of the defences of Harfleur, but this graffito inside the church of St Martin may give some impression, although with artistic license. (Anne Curry)

The *routiers*

Generally speaking, civilians were in a more protected position when conflict was between royal armies. But even then, the good behaviour of soldiers could not be guaranteed. Indeed, the Jacquerie of 1358 had its immediate cause in a group of the Dauphin's soldiers installing themselves in the fortified abbey of Saint-Leu and ignoring their master's recent order that 'no soldier take, pillage or rob our subjects of corn, wine or any other victuals'.

But the people of France were much more vulnerable when they were exposed to the bands of *routiers*. There can be little doubt that had it not been for the Anglo-French war, the problem of the *routiers* would not have arisen. It had generated a great need for soldiers, more

Ci puse de la bataille a meaux
en brie ou les Jacques furet
desconfitz par le cote de foiy
~ le captal de Beus. ~ est
iiii. xx. vi. Chapitre.

chalons que la duchesse de
normandie ~ la duchesse
dorleans et bien .m̃. dames
~ damoyselles et le duc dor
leans aussi estoient en

The war failures of the French in the 1350s stimulated popular rebellion in the early summer of 1358, known as the Jacquerie. The image is a late 15th-century portrayal of its suppression. (Photo by Fine Art Images/Heritage Images via Getty Images)

than ever before, but from time to time such men found themselves without paid employment, especially in the aftermath of Brétigny, although the civil war between the Dauphin and Charles de Navarre in the late 1350s had already generated a lawless soldiery prone to waging what was essentially their own war.

Such men were predominantly French but included English and Spanish amongst their number. Interestingly, their organisation often aped that of the formal military structures, in the 'Great Companies' which generated their own war leaders prepared to punish, often savagely, their own men. The raiding practices of the royal armies were tempting to copy – fast-moving, exciting, with easy gains, and a relatively low chance of having to fight against other soldiers. Living off the civilian population was unchallenged at times when central authority was weak. As noted earlier, civilians were a soft target with little in the way of defence, although Nicholas Wright has emphasized the solidarity generated in their attempts to resist. As he notes, in the Jacquerie the peasants of Saint-Leu were moved by the fact that the Dauphin's order had encouraged them to act against soldiers who misbehaved:

> and if soldiers do pillage, we wish and command that anyone may resist them by any method which seems best to them, and to call for help from neighbouring villages by the sound of bells. *(Order of March 1357 by the Dauphin Charles)*

It was essentially the problem of the *routiers* that led Charles V to restructure his army in the 1360s and 1370s. But it is important to remember that these companies were also from time to time recruited into royal service, not least for activities in Spain in the 1360s and in the invasion of English-held lands after 1369. By the end of the century, employment was also being found further afield, most notably in Italy.

There was a danger of the problem resurfacing in the fourth phase of the war, but not with the same scale or geographical extent as in the previous century. The English had brought in several thousand more soldiers in the mid-1430s, but reduced the garrison establishment again from the early 1440s. This generated the problem of 'men of no retinue or garrison' who were living off the land (*vivans sur le pais*) on the fringes of society. They were a useful pool of manpower on which the English could draw when vacancies arose in garrisons: indeed, their presence explains why such vacancies could be filled very quickly.

The problem of demobilization was also realized by the French. After the truce of Tours, English and French acted co-operatively in rounding up unemployed soldiers of both sides for a campaign under the Dauphin Louis in Switzerland. Later, the English ordered all of their unemployed soldiers to gather south of Argentan. Some were found garrison posts; those with crafts and lands were ordered to return to them. But all the rest, English, Welsh or Irish, who were found 'not suitable for arms' were marched under guard to Cherbourg and Barfleur in order to be shipped back to England.

Raids on southern England

Raids on England can be compared with the effect of *chevauchées* in France, for they too were conducted against soft civilian targets and were difficult to respond to effectively. By the time the shire levies were called out and despatched to the coast, the sea-borne raiders, often in oared ships, had moved on to their next target. Sea-borne raids also went for soft targets, with attacks on merchant shipping. The inhabitants of England had not experienced this style of war before, and had little defence against it at the outset of the war.

The raids, or even the threat of them, had a damaging psychological effect. At Friston and East Dean in Sussex, it was reported in 1341 that men did not dare to cultivate their lands 'for fear of the Normans'. A recent study has suggested that it was the rural poor of the south-east who suffered most from the fear and impact of raids, for the wealthy had better defences and enough capital to redeem losses. Indeed, the lack of defence afforded by the crown was certainly a factor in Kentish involvement in the Peasants' Revolt of 1381.

Kent felt the impact of the war in other ways too. The produce of its coastal areas was often reserved for the provisioning of Calais. The latter lay in such an infertile area and often housed such a large garrison – 1,000 or more – that it needed constant resupply from England. This was not popular in the county as it created artificial shortages and higher prices. The crown was notoriously slow too in paying for the food it requisitioned for Calais or indeed for anywhere else. There was certainly much complaint early in the war against the king's rights of purveyance – essentially rights of pre-emption, which often resulted in low prices to producers and considerable delays in payments being made. Parliamentary protest led to limitations on the king's rights in the 1350s. Subsequently the crown tended to use contractors to raise its supplies. Generally speaking, the issue was less pronounced in the 15th century when armies could be fed within the occupied territories, but the problem never went away fully.

Kent and Sussex also expressed annoyance in a petition to Parliament in 1429 about the quartering of soldiers, asking that they should not take food without paying for it and that, to improve discipline, soldiers' wages should be distributed before they arrived in the area. It is not surprising, therefore, that the same counties should be amongst those complaining in 1442 about robberies, rape, extortion and violence committed by the soldiery.

The raid on Southampton on 5 October 1338 provides us with a useful case study. At this point, the only defence of the southern and western waterfronts was the gating of streets. (The ability to close off streets was a common policy in French towns too in an effort to keep local order.) There had been no need for defences in the past, and warehouses and houses fronted directly on to the quayside. The raid was carried out on a Sunday when the townspeople were at Mass. There can be no doubt of the level of damage caused. The houses of the wealthy in French Street were burned out and lay unoccupied for several years, only being redeveloped towards the end of the century. Over 40 per cent of the properties belonging to the hospital of God's House seem to have been destroyed, leading to a considerable fall in rent income. A licence to appropriate churches granted later to the priory of St Denys noted that even the charters and other muniments held by the priory had been destroyed by the French. Southampton also suffered long-term decline as Italian merchants transferred their custom to Bristol for the next few years. The town had also been important in the importation of Gascon wine, a trade that more than any other reveals the impact of war.

Clearly there was a need for the fortifications of Southampton to be strengthened, and not least for

After a French raid in 1338, walls were built to protect the western side of the town of Southampton, being erected in front of existing houses and warehouses. (AmandaLewis/ Getty Images)

walls to be built along the southern and western sides of the town. These were finally completed by the end of the century, disrupting the earlier pattern of lanes, buildings and private quays, and blocking off direct access to the waterside. The cost had essentially fallen on the inhabitants through the levy of local taxes: in 1376 the townsmen requested the king that he should take the town under his control as they could not support the cost of the defences.

Some interesting developments are seen in the late 14th and 15th centuries as the use of gunpowder artillery increased. The West Gate of Canterbury, which was begun in 1380, is possibly the earliest building constructed with artillery defence in mind. The Catchcold Tower at Southampton was built in the early 1400s with three keyhole gunloops and a vaulted roof to take the weight of cannon. God's House Tower dates from slightly later. In the face of invasion threats in 1386, Thomas Tredington, chaplain, was installed in the castle at Southampton, not only to celebrate the divine service but also to keep the artillery because of his expertise in this area. By 1449–50, the town's gunner, 'Harry Gunner', was kept busy making chambers for the breech-loading guns common in this period, as well as buying gunstones, and 'two bags of leather for putting the gunpowder in'.

War and English trade

War, trade and international relations were highly interdependent. Communications between England and its continental holdings were completely dependent on the sea route. As Gascony was not a very fertile area, it imported much of its grain, as well as other commodities such as wool and cloth, from England. In return, it was England's main source of sweet wine, and salt also came into England from the Bay of Biscay. Friendly relations with Brittany were thus vital in ensuring the security

The Westgate of the city of Canterbury was built in 1379 and is one of the earliest English fortifications to have gunloops. (ianwool/ Getty Images)

of the route, and Breton pirates were a major problem when relations with the duchy were hostile. Flanders was England's major trading partner, but technically part of France. It is no coincidence that Edward III began his attack on Philip VI by manipulating the wool supply in order to force alliances from the Brabanters and Flemish, nor that the Flemish cloth towns of Bruges, Ypres and Ghent, so dependent upon English wool, should pursue different policies from their count. For the English, Calais became a staple port through which exports had to pass.

Later, the tenure of Flanders and an increasingly large part of the Low Countries by the dukes of Burgundy further complicated Anglo-French relations. The Anglo-Burgundian alliance was central to the success of the English in the third phase of the war, and even in the fourth phase when the duke defected to Charles VII, truces were agreed to allow commercial links between England and the Low Countries to continue, a reminder that wars in this period did not necessarily lead to the complete severance of trade. The French had important alliances too, not least those that brought them naval and military support – the Genoese in the first phase of the war, and the Castilians in the second. Raids on England were much assisted by the galleys provided as a result.

There was undoubtedly an effect on trade. A graph of the quantities of wine shipped to England, on which the crown took custom, shows a major downturn at the opening of the war. In 1335–36, 74,000 tuns had been exported from Bordeaux. The figure fell to 16,500 tuns in the following year, and to 6,000 tuns in 1348–49. The trade never fully recovered.

Another cause of economic loss for traders was the crown's right to impress merchant ships and crews. The English crown never had a large navy of its own and was dependent on impressment to provide not only transports but also warships. This cut into trading activities. Norfolk fishermen particularly resented being called out at the height of the herring season. Great Yarmouth's decline in the post-Black Death period has been traced to the disruption of shipping

God's House Tower was constructed to reinforce the defences of Southampton from 1417, with a flat roofed area to house gunpowder artillery. (Britpix / Alamy Stock Photo)

as a result of the war. Given the location of Edward III's early campaigns, it was frequently called upon to supply vessels: between 1335 and 1340 half of its merchant fleet was customarily in royal service. English wool export also certainly declined, but there was some compensation in the stimulus to domestic cloth production for export.

War and taxation in England and France

In England, the consent of the Commons in Parliament was needed for the grant of the lay subsidy. This brought the war fully within the public gaze. Whilst Parliament could not in practice refuse grants, it might impose conditions, such as the appointment of war treasurers at times when it felt that some of the taxes were being diverted to domestic purposes or into the pockets of certain officials. In 1376 and 1386, impeachments of ministers occurred where charges included peculation and the mishandling of funds for the war. The English were doing particularly badly at this stage. Efforts to raise more revenues through new taxes – the poll taxes levied on everyone over a certain age – led to the Peasants' Revolt of 1381.

Thenceforward, the English crown had to make do with its lay subsidy, which it was forced to reduce for some places in the wake of economic decline in the 1430s and 1440s. Thus the previous income of around £38,000 fell to around £30,000, with the income of taxation from the clergy showing a similar fall from £20,000 in the 14th century to £10,000–17,000 in the 15th. As Mark Ormrod has shown, revenue from customs duties fell from the 1360s onwards. Thus there can be no doubt that the kings of England were in a weaker financial position in the 15th century than they had been earlier. That they achieved so much after 1415 was due to their conquest of territory in France that enabled them to levy taxation there. When their territorial control diminished in the fourth phase of the war, they found themselves in considerable financial difficulties and unable to raise enough revenue on either side of the Channel.

In France, the Hundred Years War led to a considerable extension of the taxing powers of the crown. At the outset, tax was essentially an occasional payment in lieu of military service when the *arrière-ban* was called. From 1341 royal income was increased by virtue of the salt tax (*gabelle*), but Henneman's study of finances shows how precarious the French position remained, not least in the wake of the defeats of 1346 and 1356 when there was no choice but to call the Estates. John's ransom also prompted the levy of more hearth taxes (*fouages*) and purchase taxes (*aides* and *quatrièmes*), and was a major burden for all. Reims was forced to contribute 20,000 *écus* despite its fragile economic state in the wake of the military action of 1359, and had to borrow from Italian financiers. These loans

OVERLEAF
High taxation to support war with France led to popular rebellion in England in 1381, known as the Peasants' Revolt. (Photo by Prisma/ Universal Images Group/Hulton Fine Art/Getty Images)

were still being repaid when the city had a further burden on it for the coronation of Charles V in 1364, to the tune of over 77,000 *livres tournois*.

On his deathbed Charles V abolished the *fouage*, 'wishing to relieve the people to some degree of the taxes imposed upon them', and his son's government was soon forced to abolish the *aides* and *gabelle* too. Initial attempts to reimpose them led to popular rebellion in 1382, but the failure of the rebellion, very much connected to the victory over the Flemish rebel militias at Roosebeke in 1382, led to their re-introduction. Two years later, direct *tailles*, like the English lay subsidy, began to be imposed. In order to win support in the civil war, John the Fearless, Duke of Burgundy, abolished the *aides* in 1418; the Dauphin had little choice but to do the same in his area of control. But the demands of war forced their renewal again. By 1439, taxation was in practice permanent in the France ruled by Charles VII, and was instrumental in his setting up of what was in effect a standing army in the companies of the *ordonnance* and *francs archers*.

The French crown had the greatest potential to increase its tax revenues. Despite several false starts it succeeded in increasing its revenue during the war. Thus, whereas English royal tax income diminished over the course of the Hundred Years War, French revenues from the same source increased, about 45,000 *livres tournois* being raised in 1338, rising to 70,000 in the 1340s, and 155,000 by 1460. There was a further phenomenal rise under Louis XI, especially through the *taille*, so that his revenue in 1483 was at 450,000 *livres tournois*.

OPPOSITE
This portrait of John the Fearless, Duke of Burgundy (1371–1419), which is now in the Louvre, was produced around 1500. (Photo by Fine Art Images/ Heritage Images/ Getty Images)

HOW THE WAR ENDED
The loss of Normandy and Gascony

The end of the Hundred Years War came with the loss of Normandy in 1449–50, followed by that of Gascony in 1453. These events reflect the success of recent French military reforms, whilst also demonstrating the political and military disarray in which the English had put themselves after the truce of Tours of May 1444.

If the English intended to use the truce to fortify their position, as the Duke of Suffolk implied to the Parliament of 1445, then they went a strange way about it. They undertook defence cuts to save money, since, in time of truce, they could not ask for heavy taxation from the Norman Estates. The garrisons in Normandy were reduced from about 3,500 to 2,500 men in June 1444, and may have fallen to 2,000 by 1448. Inadequate attention was paid to the maintenance of fortifications and to the provision of artillery. Castles and towns were thus easy pickings for Charles VII after he declared war on 17 July 1449. By reducing the garrisons, the English had lost the capacity to send detachments into the field. The expeditionary forces despatched from England in 1450 were too little, too late.

The French, on the other hand, capitalized on the truce. Building on the arrangements made by Charles V, the king created more companies of cavalry to produce 12,000 men. Each company contained 100 'lances', each containing a man-at-arms, a coutiller, a page, two archers (largely crossbowmen, although the French were starting to make greater use of the longbow), and a *valet de guerre*. To these he added, by means of an order issued in 1448, the obligation that each parish should provide one archer, producing a total of 8,000 *francs archers*. Together these constituted an army on permanent standby, although only paid when in active service, and still supplemented by troops raised through the *semonce des nobles* and *arrière-ban*. A strong artillery train was also developed under the direction of the Bureau brothers. Charles had also gained the important military alliance of Duke Francis of Brittany.

> We have now taken steps to ensure the safety of our kingdom in case the truce between us and our nephew of England does not bring peace. For it is right and proper that we should establish in our kingdom a number of men for its defence whom we can use in our service in time of war without having to employ those who are not our subjects … in each parish there shall be one archer who will keep himself always ready and equipped for war with a sallet, dagger, sword, bow, sheath of arrows, jerkin and a short coat of mail. *(Order of Charles VII, 28 April 1448)*

Charles cannot have been unaware of the weakness of the English defences. Henry VI had already shown himself vulnerable to pressure, for in December 1445 he had agreed to surrender Maine. Although this was intended to assist in peace negotiations, it was a foolish decision because it weakened his diplomatic position and undermined morale. English soldiers such as Osbern Mundeford could not believe that their king and commanders had agreed to it, but they had little choice but to withdraw from Maine in March 1448. The sight of demobilized soldiers and settlers drifting through Normandy can hardly have boosted the confidence of those in the garrisons of the duchy, whose own pay was increasingly erratic now that the tax

In his invasion of Normandy of 1449–50, Charles VII was able to count on the support of Francis II, Duke of Brittany, whose seal is portrayed here. (agefotostock / Alamy Stock Photo)

income was reduced, but who found their freedom of action and opportunities for booty limited by the need to observe the truce.

Under such circumstances, it seems even greater folly that the English should give the French an excuse to break the truce by capturing Fougères on 24 March 1449. This fortress lay within Brittany. Thus the attack on it served to bring the duke closer to support of Charles VII. The English had hoped to do the opposite: their plan had been to put pressure on Duke Francis to release from captivity his pro-English brother, Giles.

The assault on Fougères was a gamble. War leaders tried to argue that it was an independent action carried out by an Arragonese mercenary who had long been in their pay, Sir François l'Arragonais. (L'Arragonais is himself a fascinating example of the kind of soldier the war produced – holder of the Garter, but later master of the Duke of Burgundy's artillery and the recipient of a pension from Louis XI.) Research has shown that

Osbern Mundeford

Osbern Mundeford provides us with a good example of a soldier fighting for English interests in France. His father had served in the Agincourt campaign. He himself developed a career in southern Normandy, being based at Fresnay-sur-Sarthe, and also serving in the conquest of Maine. He was also involved in military administration, being responsible for discipline and the provision of victuals in Fresnay. We also find him on one occasion reinforcing Caen, and also on a raid into Picardy after the defection of the Burgundians. By the mid-1440s he was combining military and administrative offices as captain and bailli of Le Mans. He found himself in a difficult position in December 1445 when ordered to surrender the city to the French king, and questioned the decision until forced by the arrival in France of Edmund Beaufort, Duke of Somerset, as Henry VI's royal lieutenant.

Mundeford subsequently became Somerset's treasurer of Normandy. When Charles VII reopened the war in July 1449 he was collecting revenues and foodstuffs for English garrisons between Vernon and Mantes but was captured by the French at Pont-Audemer on 12 August. Fortunately he was helped by his fellow soldier and brother-in-law Andrew Trollope. When Trollope surrendered Fresnay to the French in March 1450 he was able to include in the surrender terms that Mundeford should be released from his captivity. He went on to join the garrison at Calais where he served as marshal alongside Trollope in the early 1450s.

the plan was officially endorsed: the garrisons of Lower Normandy had been reinforced shortly before, with a campaign in Brittany perhaps intended. The taking of Fougères might have assisted the English military and diplomatic position had it been followed up by further action, but instead l'Arragonais found himself without aid and was forced to evacuate the place.

The truce had already shown itself a fragile beast, being renewed only for short periods, with many disputes over supposed infractions. It is clear that Charles was keen for an opportunity to attack (his readiness for invasion and his diplomatic dealings with Brittany give sound proof of this), but as the English were so obviously unprepared, it was suicidal that they should give him the excuse he needed.

In Normandy there was a change of leadership. The lieutenant-general, Richard, Duke of York, had been recalled at the end of 1445. A year later, Edmund Beaufort, Duke of Somerset, replaced him, but he did not cross until May 1448. He was certainly not lacking in experience or ability, and tried hard to improve military discipline and to deal with the complaints of inhabitants. He was fully aware of the vulnerability of the duchy, as his letter read in Parliament in the spring of 1449 makes clear.

> If war should occur, which God forbid, Normandy is no way sufficient in itself to offer resistance against the great might of the enemy. For there is no place in the King's obedience provided for in terms of repairs, ordnance, or any kind of artillery ... almost all places have fallen into such ruin that even were they to be stocked up with men and ordnance, they could not be defended. *(Roll of Parliament)*

Somerset also said that the Estates of Normandy could bear no more taxation. But Parliament was reluctant to vote English money. Its suggestion that those English granted lands in the duchy should donate part of their revenues was a good example of how little those at home knew of the realities of the situation: many settlers had lost their lands after 1435 or else seen incomes diminished by war and by an economic downturn. The situation was not assisted by the king's lack of enthusiasm, or by growing political machinations, which encouraged many leading captains to stay in England.

The loss of the duchy further exacerbated political problems at home. A scapegoat had to be found. Suffolk thus found himself impeached early in 1450 whilst the towns and castles of the duchy continued to fall. Sentenced to exile, he was lynched on his way out of England. Popular disquiet that the duchy fell so easily and without the English government offering resistance is also demonstrated by Cade's rebellion in May–June

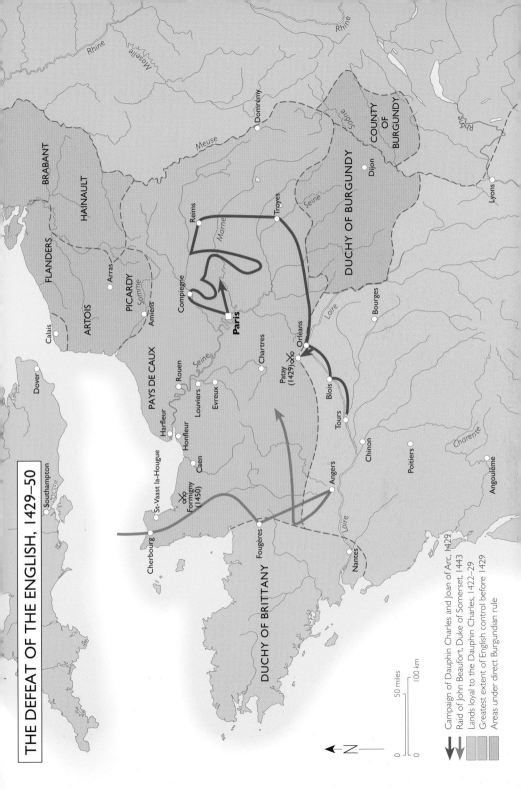

THE DEFEAT OF THE ENGLISH, 1429–50

Rhine

Rhine

Moselle

Meuse

BRABANT

HAINAULT

Domrémy

COUNTY
OF
BURGUNDY

FLANDERS

Seine

Rhône

Arras

PICARDY

Reims

Marne

Troyes

Dijon

DUCHY OF BURGUNDY

Lyons

ARTOIS

Somme

Calais

Amiens

Compiègne

Bourges

Loire

Dover

PAYS DE CAUX

Rouen

Seine

Paris

Chartres

Orléans

Harfleur

Louviers

Evreux

Patay
(1429)

Blois

Southampton

Ste-Vaast la-Hougue

Caen

Honfleur

Tours

Chinon

Poitiers

Charente

Angoulême

Cherbourg

Formigny
(1450)

Angers

Loire

Fougères

DUCHY OF BRITTANY

Nantes

N

0   50 miles
0   100 km

Campaign of Dauphin Charles and Joan of Arc, 1429
Raid of John Beaufort, Duke of Somerset, 1443
Lands loyal to the Dauphin Charles, 1422–29
Greatest extent of English control before 1429
Areas under direct Burgundian rule

1450. Amongst other things, the rebels urged that the 'traitors' responsible should be brought to book. In the years that followed, York, who had himself lost much land in Normandy, stressed the culpability of Somerset. This was in effect the origin of the dispute that culminated in the first battle of the Wars of the Roses at St Albans in 1455, where Somerset met his death.

The loss of Normandy was swift and largely unchallenged. Places had already started to fall even before the declaration of war. Pont-de-l'Arche, an important defence for Rouen, was captured on 16 May 1449 with the aid of a merchant of Louviers. The willingness of the inhabitants of Normandy to betray their towns to the French king is revealed on many subsequent occasions over the next year, reminding us that military outcomes were as dependent upon local opinion as on the effectiveness of troops. It is easy to say that the Normans had simply been waiting for liberation from the foreign occupier, and that they had only been kept in check by English military presence, but the issue of loyalty was much more complex and varied, and much affected by the desire of civilians to preserve their own livelihoods. For them, the power worthy of support was the one that could maintain the peace. Before 1449 this had been the English, now it was the French.

Normandy was invaded from the north-east by the counts of Saint-Pol and Eu, from the east along the Seine by the Count of Dunois and Duke of Alençon and later the king along the Seine, and from the south-west by the Duke of Brittany and his uncle, Arthur de Richemont, a veteran of Agincourt. They swept everything before them in a *blitzkrieg*. Scarcely anywhere held out for longer than a few days. Once Rouen surrendered on 29 October at the behest of its inhabitants, the English cause was irredeemable. Charles *'le très victorieux'* (the most victorious) was welcomed into the Norman capital and elsewhere in triumph.

By January 1450, only Caen, Bayeux, Falaise and the Cotentin remained in English hands. Here a brief revival occurred when English reinforcements under

OPPOSITE
The Anglo-French truce of 1444 was undermined by an English attack in March 1449 on the castle of Fougères, which lay on the Breton side of the frontier of Lower Normandy. (prill/ Getty Images)

OPPOSITE
Edmund Beaufort,
Duke of Somerset,
was lieutenant-
general for the
English when
Charles VII declared
war in August
1449. He could do
little to prevent
French conquest
of Normandy. (The
History Collection /
Alamy Stock Photo)

Sir Thomas Kyriell arrived at Cherbourg, but a decisive blow was dealt at the battle of Formigny on 15 April, where the English were emphatically defeated. This battle is significant because its outcome depended on the Count of Clermont's judicious use of gunfire to draw the larger English army out of its defensive position. The potential power of the artillery train built up by Charles had already been apparent at the capture of Mantes, but there the inhabitants had decided to surrender to avoid destruction of the walls on which they had lavished much taxation. After Formigny, the French moved inexorably up the Cotentin. On 12 August, the last English-held place, Cherbourg, surrendered.

Charles now turned his attention to Gascony with an army of 7,000, many of whom had served in Normandy, knowing that he had already received offers of support from nobility in the duchy. Bordeaux surrendered to Dunois on 30 June 1451. The English raised an army of 3,000 under Sir Richard Woodville, a veteran of the Norman campaigns, but the dispatch of the force was postponed from its original date of 18 October 1450, and it is unlikely that any troops reached the duchy. By August it had been cancelled because of fears of a French invasion of south-west England and the need to send reinforcements to Calais.

In the following year there were competing interests: Calais and the Channel Islands; an armed fleet at sea; and relief to Gascony. An army of 5,000 was raised under Lord Talbot for the sea, but then sent to Gascony, where it recaptured Bordeaux on 20 October 1452 with the aid of partisans. The French had expected Talbot to land in Normandy. Many of the cavalry companies were still stationed there, and the *francs archers* had also been summoned to the coast. Gascony had thus been left relatively undefended.

A relief force of 2,000 was sent from England in the spring of 1453, but another due in August never crossed. Charles was able to deploy a force of 8,000. Talbot was defeated and killed at the battle of Castillon on 17 July. Here he used the customary tactic of an

Cy commence le .ij.e liure lequel contient en soy. xlij. chapittres
Du premier il parle de la prinse de fougieres par les anglois
et de la prinse du pont de lartse par les francois conquinat sains
mauxxain et saint seleberoy en beauuaisie Chapitre .XI.

U tempe que   Et que se duc de sombreset
les tribulla   estoit capittaine et gouuer
tions et en   neur du pays de northma
bies dittes   die et de tous ceulx qui te
au precedent   noient en france et autre
volume requi   pays villes et chasteaulx,
noient entre les princes—   tenans le parrty du roy dan
du royaulme dangleterre   gleterre par lacordance

The island of Mont-Saint-Michel, with its fortified monastery, was the only place in Normandy which the English did not capture, despite sieges laid by land and sea. (Krzysztof Belczyński, Flickr, CC BY-SA 2.0)

attack on foot. But on this occasion it was the English who were mown down by French arrow fire, and also by gunshot. Bordeaux held out for a further three months, but without the possibility of aid from England the city had to surrender on 19 October 1453. The English now had only Calais.

CONCLUSIONS AND CONSEQUENCES
A defining moment in history

We might expect a war to end with some kind of peace settlement that reflected and reinforced the victory of one side over the other. There was no negotiated settlement for the end of the Hundred Years War. Calais remained in English hands until 1558, and it was not until the Treaty of Amiens of 1801 that the title 'king of France' was abandoned: by then, of course, France no longer had a monarch.

A recurrent theme in the history of Europe between the late-15th century and the mid-19th century was Anglo-French hostility. But 1453 has much to recommend it as both the end of an era and the end of a war. It marked the final loss of the lands in south-west France which had been held by English kings since the 12th century. If we accept that these lands were the *real* long-term cause of Anglo-French hostilities, then their loss was a major turning point in Anglo-French relations. Never again were the English able to support a meaningful claim to the French throne by virtue of a major presence in France.

The fact that Normandy had been lost only a few years earlier was most significant. The occupation of Normandy had given the English control of one of the wealthiest and most strategically significant areas of France. And it had been lost all too easily. Worse still, it proved impossible to effect any recovery of any of the lost lands. Resources had to be poured into the defence of Calais. Henry VI's descent into madness in the summer of 1453, which created governmental paralysis and further fanned divisions, not least between Somerset and York, towards civil war, was no doubt a major factor in why no effort was made to invade France again after 1453, although a shortage of money was also influential. The enormity of the task was self-evident, not least because Charles VII, at first worried that the English would return, had ensured the firm defence of his conquests, and had encouraged attacks on the English coasts and shipping.

French historians have made it quite clear that Charles's authority was much boosted by the recovery of Normandy and Gascony. So emphatic were the victories that he chose to exploit them for propaganda purposes and his loyal people followed in his wake. Economic recovery was slow but was assisted by the fact that the recoveries had been easy and not physically destructive.

> With the heart of a lion and courage of a prince he entered Normandy with a large army and by sieges, battles and surprise attacks as well as other means he drove you English out in one season, which is a very short time indeed. He has left you not a single place ... conquering all that you and your king Henry had conquered in thirty-three years. (*Treatise known as* The Debate of the Heralds of England and France, *c. 1455*)

All in all, therefore, the French emerged stronger from the war and the English weaker. Even though both suffered civil war in the decades that followed, it was in England that royal authority was dealt a major blow in the Wars of the Roses, whereas both Charles VII and his son Louis XI began the road to absolutism. Their military reforms and increased use of gunpowder artillery, backed up by a further expansion in royal authority and taxing capacity, paved the way for the large armies of the early modern period and in particular for French intervention

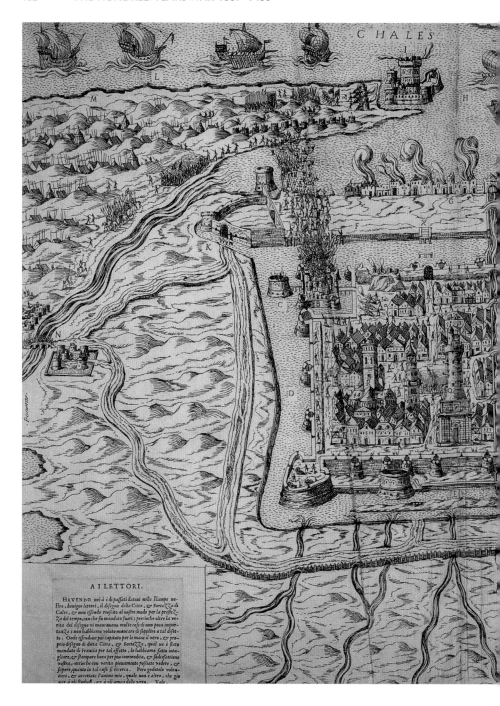

A I LETTORI.

HAVENDO noi à i dì paſſati datoui nelle ſtampe no-
ſtre, benigni lettori, il diſegno della Citta, & Fortezza di
Cales, & non eſſendo riuſcito al noſtro modo per la preſtez-
za del tempo, can che fu mandato fuori i percioche oltre la ve-
rità del diſegno vi mancauano molte coſe di non poca impor-
tanza ; non habbiamo voluto mancare di ſupplire a tal diſet-
to. Onde eſſendone poi capitato per le mani il vero, & pro-
prio diſegno di detta Citta, & Fortezza, qual ne è ſtato
mandato di Francia per tal effetto, lo habbiamo fatto inta-
gliare, & ſtampare hora per piu commodita, & ſodisfattione
voſtra, accioche con verita pienamente poſſiate vedere, &
ſapere, quanto in tal caſo ſi ricerca. Pero godetelo volen-
tieri, & accettate l'animo mio, quale non è altro, che gia
war à gli ſtudioſi, & à gli amici delle virtu. Vale.

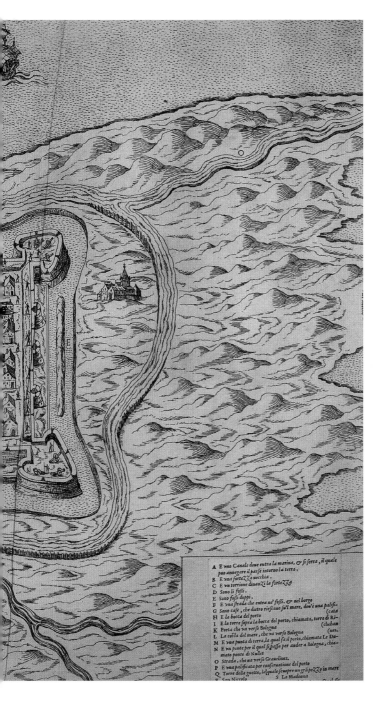

Calais remained in English hands until January 1558 when it was recaptured by Francis de Lorraine, Duke of Guise. (Album / Alamy Stock Photo)

OPPOSITE
A 17th-century
portrait of Louis
XI, housed at his
favourite château
of Plessis-lès-Tours.
Louis successfully
restored the
authority of the
French crown.
(The Picture Art
Collection / Alamy
Stock Photo)

in Italy at the turn of the century. In England, the armies imploded on themselves. Many who served Lancaster and York in the Wars of the Roses had been in the English army in France. We saw two examples earlier in Trollope and Mundeford.

From the historian's privileged position of hindsight, there can be no doubt that the end of the Hundred Years War, and indeed the whole war itself, were defining moments in English and French history. The war had been by far the most long-standing – and the most militarily and politically significant – conflict in western Europe in the later Middle Ages. It had involved virtually every other state at one time or another. It had divided France twice, in 1360 and in 1420 – events that did much to embitter the French towards the English. Their very freedom and existence were under threat.

The claim to the French throne was perhaps at the forefront of English ambitions only from the assassination of John the Fearless in 1419, but its very use since 1340 had elevated the war to a new status – no longer a war between vassal and sovereign but between two sovereigns. In such a scenario it is not surprising that ideas of national identity hardened and insults were traded between the two nations. They remained 'wars of kings' throughout, but the nature of the fighting, which targeted civilians in a way that they were powerless to resist, and the level of the taxation burden made them also 'wars of peoples'. The expression 'society at war' does indeed seem appropriate.

There can be no doubt of the war's importance in military terms. Because of its length and intensity, and the fact that it was often waged in several areas simultaneously, it had prompted an increase in the number of men for whom soldiering was a primary occupation. It had persuaded the English and French to increase the proportion of archers in their armies in order to generate numerical presence and effective 'human mass artillery'. It had increased demands for weapons, armour and fortifications, and had no doubt encouraged the development of gunpowder artillery.

The battle of Agincourt is traditionally believed to have been fought between the villages of Azincourt and Tramecourt, but this location is contested. (Peter Hoskins)

In this, the English had not moved as quickly as the French, being too complacent in their defence of Normandy and Gascony, and being constrained by the difficulties of holding lands overseas. But it had generated in Normandy what was essentially an English standing army, which was then outmatched by Charles VII's military advances of the mid-1440s.

The Hundred Years War saw many forms of warfare, but a final note can be sounded about its major battles. It has become fashionable to downplay the significance of battles and to bring to mind that they were the least common form of conflict. None of the battles of the war was decisive – no form of medieval warfare could be decisive, as the scale was too small and the impact too localized. But Sluys, Crécy, Poitiers, La Rochelle, Agincourt, Patay and Formigny all had marked catalytic effects on the course of the conflict in a way that no other forms of action did or could have done. For contemporaries these were the defining moments, and clear testimony of the seriousness and bitterness with which the Hundred Years War was fought.

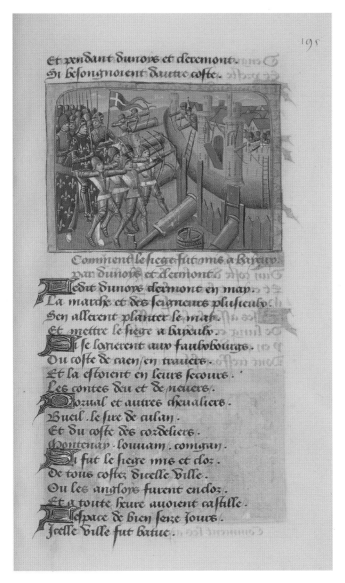

After defeating the English at the battle of Formigny, the French went on to besiege the last remaining towns in English hands. Matthew Gough held out at Bayeux until 16 May but was forced to surrender in the face of threats of bombardment. (Bibliothèque Nationale de France)

CHRONOLOGY

Second phase

1369	Charles V declares Edward III's lands confiscate
1369–74	French recover all save Gascony and Calais
1372	English fleet defeated off La Rochelle
1382	French defeat Flemish townsmen at Roosebeke
1389	Truce agreed, extended in 1396 to 28 years

Third phase

1412	Henry IV sends army to assist Armagnacs
1415	Henry V takes Harfleur and defeats French at Agincourt
1417–19	Conquest of Normandy
1419	Assassination of John, Duke of Burgundy
1420	Treaty of Troyes makes Henry V heir and regent of France
1423	Anglo-Burgundian victory at Cravant
1424	English victory at Verneuil
1425–28	English take Maine and move towards Loire

Fourth phase

1429	French raise siege of Orléans and defeat English at Patay; Charles VII crowned at Reims
1431	Henry VI crowned in Paris
1435–36	Burgundy defects to France; the pays de Caux and Paris fall to French
1444	Truce of Tours

The end of the war

1449	English take Fougères; French begin reconquest of Normandy
1450	French victory at Formigny
1451	Gascony falls to the French
1453	English defeated at Castillon

FURTHER READING

Allmand, C. T., *Lancastrian Normandy: The History of a Medieval Occupation 1415–1450*, 1983.

Allmand, C. T., *The Hundred Years War: England and France at War c.1300–c.1450*, 1988.

Allmand, C. T., *Society at War: The Experience of England and France during the Hundred Years War*, new edition, 1998.

Ambuhl, R., *Prisoners of War in the Hundred Years War: Ransom Culture in the Late Middle Ages*, 2013.

Ayton, A., *Knights and Warhorses: Military Service and the English Aristocracy under Edward III*, 1994.

Ayton, A., and Preston, P., *The Battle of Crécy 1346*, 2005.

Barber, R., *Edward, Prince of Wales and Aquitaine. A Biography of the Black Prince*, rev. edn. 1996

Barker, J., *Conquest. The English Kingdom of France*, 2009.

Bell, A. R., Curry, A., King, A., and Simpkin, D., *The Soldier in Later Medieval England*, 2013

Contamine, P., *War in the Middle Ages,* English edition trans. M. Jones, 1984.

Curry, A., ed., *Agincourt 1415: Henry V, Sir Thomas Erpingham and the Triumph of the English Archers*, 2000.

Curry, A., *The Battle of Agincourt: Sources and Interpretations*, 2000.

Curry, A., *The Hundred Years War*, rev. edn., 2003.

Curry, A., *Agincourt. A New History,* rev. edn., 2015.

Curry, A., ed., *The Hundred Years War Revisited*, 2019.

Curry, A. and Hughes, M., eds, *Arms, Armies and Fortifications in the Hundred Years War*, 1994.

Curry, A., and Mercer, M., *The Battle of Agincourt. The Illustrated Companion*, 2015.

DeVries, K., *Medieval Military Technology*, 1992

DeVries, K., *Infantry Warfare in the Early Fourteenth Century*, 1996.

Fowler, K., *Medieval Mercenaries*, Vol. 1: *The Great Companies*, 2001.

Friel, I., *The Good Ship: Ships, Shipbuilding and Technology in England 1200–1520*, 1995.

Froissart, Jean, *Chronicles*, ed. G. Brereton, 1968.

Hoskins, P., *In the Steps of the Black Prince. The Road to Poitiers, 1355-1356*, 2011.

Hoskins, P., *Siege Warfare during the Hundred Years War*, 2018.

Jones, M., *Ducal Brittany 1364–1399*, 1970.

Jones, M. and Vale, M. G. A., eds, *England and her Neighbours in the Middle Ages*, 1989.

Keen, M., *The Laws of War in the Late Middle Ages*, 1965.

Keen, M., ed., *Medieval Warfare: A History*, 1999.

Lambert, C., *Shipping the Medieval Military: English Maritime Logistics in the Fourteenth Century*, 2011.

Lucas, H. S., *The Low Countries and the Hundred Years War*, 1929.

Maddern, M., *The Black Prince and the Grande Chevauché of 1355*, 2018

Nicolle, D., *Medieval Warfare Sources Book*, Vol. 1: *Warfare in Western Christendom*, 1995.

Palmer, J. J. N., *England, France and Christendom, 1377–1399*, 1972.

Pernoud, R. and Clin, Marie-Veronique, *Joan of Arc: Her Story*, 2000.

Perroy, E., *The Hundred Years War*, 1951.

Pollard, A. J., *John Talbot and the War in France 1426–1453*, 1983.

Prestwich, M., *Armies and Warfare in the Middle Ages: The English Experience*, 1996.

Rogers, C. J., *War Cruel and Sharp: English Strategy under Edward III, 1327–1360*, 2000.

Rogers, C. J., ed., *The Wars of Edward III*, 2000.

Small, G., *Late Medieval France*, 2009.

Sumption, J., *The Hundred Years War*, Vol. 1: *Trial by Battle*, 1990.

Sumption, J., *The Hundred Years War*, Vol. 2: *Trial by Fire*, 1999.

Sumption, J., *The Hundred Years War*, Vol. 3: *Divided Houses*, 2009.

Sumption, J., *The Hundred Years War*, Vol. 4: *Cursed Kings*, 2015.

Vale, M. G. A., *English Gascony 1399–1413*, 1970.

Vale, M. G. A., *The Angevin Legacy and the Hundred Years War 1250–1340*, 1990, republished as *The Origins of the Hundred Years War*, 1996.

Wright, N., *Knights and Peasants: The Hundred Years War in the French Countryside*, 1998.

INDEX